Advance praise for *Let's Get Real or Let's Not Play*

"*Let's Get Real or Let's Not Play* is a must read for every person involved in a client service business. It is a "go-to" play book for every consultant in all industries."
—Rick Wellner, CEBS Senior Vice President,
Aon Global, Aon Consulting

"*Let's Get Real or Let's Not Play* correctly positions the art of selling as the art of relationship building. It's a simple, powerful, and practical way to grow a business."   **—John Jantsch, author of *Duct Tape Marketing***

"If you want to positively differentiate yourself from your competition, read *Let's Get Real or Let's Not Play*. Most of all, this book will help you help your clients succeed, and your success will grow."
—Jeff Renzi, Executive Vice President,
Global Sales & Marketing, Perot Systems

"*Let's Get Real or Let's Not Play* should be required study for any sales professional, at any level, who is committed to increasing sales proficiency and tangible order production. Mahan and Randy have done a great job explaining the fundamentals of the sales process, based on recognizing client needs and building client trust and acceptance."
—Armen A. Manoogian, CEO, United Business Technologies

"Selling is a complex, competitive and challenging career. Mahan and Randy walk their readers through a way of thinking about their customers, which results in better solutions, customer loyalty, larger deals, and less wasted time for sales professionals and their customers."
—Jeffrey P. Kane, President, NEC Unified Solutions, Inc.

"*Let's Get Real or Let's Not Play* isn't for the casual, opportunistic skill-skimmer who PLAYS at sales. It's for those who need to get REAL about selling. Mahan Khalsa and Randy Illig provide the philosophy, the what-to-do and how-to-do-it, to clearly guide us through some of our toughest challenges and find breakthrough success in sales."

—**Dave Stein, CEO and Founder, ES Research Group, Inc.**

"Send *Let's Get Real or Let's Not Play* to every prospect you have—if they read it and understand the transforming message on selling and buying you have a great prospect. If they don't—save yourself a lot of time and move on!"

—**Taylor Macdonald, Vice President,
Worldwide Channels and Sales Alliance, Deltek**

"*Let's Get Real or Let's Not Play* is vital for everyone involved in B-to-B sales. The concepts and tools shared in the book will raise your awareness to new levels of understanding, thinking, trust, and influence to create the best possible foundation for working together with clients to create extraordinary success for both parties."

—**Greg Boyd, President, MIS Group**

"*Let's Get Real or Let's Not Play* provides a powerful process and set of tools for moving away from non-productive sales activities and toward "getting real," to truly understand clients and create value. If you want to consistently win and retain clients, read this book."

—**Ralph Oliva, Executive Director, Institute for the Study of
Business Markets, SMEAL College of Business, Penn State**

"*Let's Get Real or Let's Not Play* is *the* how-to-do-it book that will generate sales."

—**Phil Clark, Senior Vice President,
Global Sales and Marketing, Invensys Process Systems**

"*Let's Get Real or Let's Not Play* gets to the heart of how to become world-class trusted advisors who genuinely help clients succeed. The approach and tools found in the book can make a big difference in any company that wants to be known for providing value to their clients and not just billing services."

—**Ann Lathrop, Executive-in-Charge of Marketing Development
and Sales, Crowe Chizek and Company LLC**

LET'S GET REAL
OR LET'S NOT PLAY

LET'S GET REAL OR LET'S NOT PLAY

TRANSFORMING THE BUYER / SELLER RELATIONSHIP

MAHAN KHALSA
and RANDY ILLIG

PORTFOLIO

PORTFOLIO
Published by the Penguin Group
Penguin Group (USA) Inc., 375 Hudson Street, New York, New York 10014, U.S.A. • Penguin Group
(Canada), 90 Eglinton Avenue East, Suite 700, Toronto, Ontario, Canada M4P 2Y3 (a division of Pearson
Penguin Canada Inc.) • Penguin Books Ltd, 80 Strand, London WC2R 0RL, England • Penguin Ire-
land, 25 St. Stephen's Green, Dublin 2, Ireland (a division of Penguin Books Ltd) • Penguin Books Aus-
tralia Ltd, 250 Camberwell Road, Camberwell, Victoria 3124, Australia (a division of Pearson Australia
Group Pty Ltd) • Penguin Books India Pvt Ltd, 11 Community Centre, Panchsheel Park, New Delhi –
110 017, India • Penguin Group (NZ), 67 Apollo Drive, Rosedale, North Shore 0632, New Zealand
(a division of Pearson New Zealand Ltd) • Penguin Books (South Africa) (Pty) Ltd, 24 Sturdee Avenue,
Rosebank, Johannesburg 2196, South Africa

Penguin Books Ltd, Registered Offices:
80 Strand, London WC2R 0RL, England

This revised and updated edition published in 2008 by
Portfolio, a member of Penguin Group (USA) Inc.

3   5   7   9   10   8   6   4   2

Copyright © FranklinCovey Co., 1999, 2008
All rights reserved

Artwork by Blaine C. Lee, blaineWorks Graphic Design and Think Tank Creative Consortium

LIBRARY OF CONGRESS CATALOGING IN PUBLICATION DATA
ISBN 978-1-59184-226-2

Printed in the United States of America
Set in Minion
Designed by Vicky Hartman

Contents

Foreword

by STEPHEN R. COVEY

When it comes to sales and growing revenues, companies find themselves under enormous pressure to sell better and faster—and to reach greater levels of performance. On top of that, global competition is fierce and buyers are increasingly savvy, putting pressure on sellers to sell more for less. Faced with this environment, many companies, even the most successful ones, are finding that they can't keep selling as usual—that something has to change for them to preserve their margins, cut down their sales cycles and costs, and grow long-term business partnerships.

I believe the time is well overdue for companies and everyone involved in the sales process—whether it's the CEO, sales manager, or salesperson—to break through dysfunctional selling and buying habits and adopt an entirely new paradigm and framework that will take sales to a higher level.

In *Let's Get Real or Let's Not Play*, you will find a new paradigm for sales greatness along with the habits that will lead you to highly effective selling in a competitive global environment. I believe this book's framework, principles, and how-to instructions provide the necessary process, methodology, tools, and skills for creating and sustaining superior sales performance. There is no other sales book like it, and I have great confidence in its enduring principles for long-term sales success.

I have profound admiration for Mahan Khalsa and how he has, with humility and courage over the years, challenged the old conventions of buying and selling. In their place, he has created a principle-centered, breakthrough way of helping sellers and buyers bridge their fears and mistrust of one another and break down the many dysfunctional practices that have arisen from this lack of trust. In developing the "Helping Clients Succeed" mind-set, tool set, and skill set central to *Let's Get Real or Let's Not Play*, Mahan has given the business world a powerful, commonsense (yet not common practice) way for sellers and buyers to communicate, think, and act with authenticity, trust, and integrity to reach win-win results.

Mahan's approach says the role of salespeople is to passionately focus on clients to help them succeed. Simply put, the more that salespeople concentrate on their clients' numbers, the more their own numbers go up. Furthermore, if this process takes place in an authentic and competent way, then salespeople are transformed into trusted business advisors in the client's eyes. This, in turn, builds a synergistic partnership for future business, taking sales to a higher level—in both high-integrity, trustworthy, win-win relationships, and increased business opportunities and revenue.

Now, in this book, Mahan and his colleague Randy Illig provide a complete sales process and framework to dramatically raise sales performance and productivity along the entire sales cycle. From filling the pipeline with the right new opportunities, to qualifying and advancing opportunities, and to closing business, sales organizations will find success by following the process in this book. And best of all, they can increase sales today in a way that creates even more sales in the future.

I believe that in *Let's Get Real or Let's Not Play*, sales leaders, teams, or individual salespersons will find the answers to the daily challenges they face. It will help a leader by giving him or her—and thus the organization—the necessary paradigm, processes, and skills to focus not on quick fixes but on principles of enduring sales success. It is critical for the leadership ranks to rethink the way they approach sales and how they manage their teams. Mahan and Randy give sales leaders what they need to build and sustain a sales culture of greatness—one that unleashes the potential of salespeople toward proactively helping clients succeed and, thereby, toward finding their own success and fulfillment, not just in the short term but consistently, year after year.

On the team or individual level, salespeople will find a new way of thinking about their role and how they can dramatically improve their performance. At first glance, many of the principles in this book seem counterintuitive, but they challenge salespeople to look at things differently and grow in their abilities to help clients succeed. Take, for example, "Move off the Solution." Can you imagine a salesperson not chomping at the bit to start talking about his or her solution and how great it is? Yet to have clients feel understood and valued, salespeople have to follow the principle of seeking first to understand, then to be understood. This requires salespeople to talk less and listen more. They can do this by first moving off the solution, asking effective questions, and *listening*.

In *Let's Get Real or Let's Not Play*, salespeople will learn how to create an honest and open environment that allows clients to feel safe enough to share what they think, believe, and value. The trust that is created through this process enables clients to actually partner with salespeople to co-develop a business case and a solution that exactly meets the client's needs in a mutually beneficial way. This is true win-win!

I have no doubt that any salesperson will feel more energized and empowered as they follow the framework provided by Mahan and Randy. Few things are more discouraging to salespeople than not making their numbers. And the more they miss their numbers, the more likely the numbers are raised and the pressure to perform increases. With the mind-set, skill set, and tool set presented in this book, salespeople will find new freedom and enjoyment in their work because they will have a proven way of engaging clients in honest, structured business conversations that help clients feel understood and valued and lead to solutions that produce measureable results.

The role of trusted business advisor is more than anything a key differentiator in our increasingly competitive, global marketplace. Those who can truly understand clients and their business issues, and deliver tangible benefits, are the ones who win more business—better and faster.

Let's Get Real or Let's Not Play is a powerful, breakthrough book. Mahan Khalsa and Randy Illig masterfully put the art and science of influence and sales on new and higher ground. Any organization looking to reengage and renew its sales force with pragmatic, disciplined, commonsense process and execution will find proven answers in this book. Mahan and Randy prove that you can indeed create win-win by focusing entirely on helping clients succeed—and create a culture of excellence in any sales organization.

This is a must-read and must-practice for anyone in sales and business development. But it is much more than that. I find Mahan's and Randy's principles for effective human interaction, trust building, critical thinking, and execution invaluable for the entire business world.

Preface

There is a story about how this book came to be in your hands. Some of you won't care about the story. You'll prefer to skip the preface and jump right into the book. After all, if the book doesn't interest you, who cares about the story? And you can always come back to the story later, should you so choose. If that is your preference, please proceed to the introduction, safe in knowing your enjoyment and use of the book won't be compromised by not reading the story behind it.

Other readers like to get a sense of the authors and their background. It gives them a context for what they are about to read. If you are of that demeanor, read on.

MY NAME IS Mahan Khalsa. My collaborator, Randy Illig, and I decided that a story is told better by one person than by two. So while the body of this book is a joint effort and written from our common voice, I am the storyteller in this preface. That seems appropriate since this particular journey begins with me and is joined by Randy along the way. To provide some balance, Randy finishes the story in the Last Words section at the end of the book.

I love selling. It encourages me to constantly grow in every facet of my being. I look forward with excitement and eager anticipation to working with clients. But I assure you, this was not always the case. Far from it.

My first encounters with selling were painful. I was working my way through college and needed a job. I took a position as a door-to-door salesman. The person who trained me made it look easy. He had a great territory, and when he knocked on the door, people would say, "John—good to see you. What do you have for me today?" I thought to myself, "I can do this!" Of course, I was assigned to the worst part of town. I would knock on the door and people would pull down their shades or scream curses at me. The routine was: knock on the door, get rejected, repeat for 50 to 100 times to get a sale. And when I finally did make a sale, I would have to deliver it a week later only to find no one home, or that they didn't have any money, or they didn't live there anymore, or they didn't want what they ordered. . . . it was brutal. It hurt a lot.

So I took another sales position. It was also door-to-door; however, it was in a city with lots of tall apartment buildings. I figured I could get my rejections more efficiently if all the doors I had to knock on were close together. All the buildings had skulls and crossbones on them that communicated death (and worse) to solicitors. The person who trained me consoled me with the two most repeated words of salespeople: "No problem!" He'd ring an apartment on the top floor of a building. The person would answer and he'd say, "Western Union!" They'd ring the buzzer and we'd trudge up to the top floor. The person would open the door and my supervisor would begin his pitch. After a couple of minutes the person would look confused and say, "I thought you were Western Union." My fearless leader would respond, "Western Union? Oh, my goodness. I'm sorry. No, I said my name is Lester Newman!" The person would slam the door in our faces, and we would proceed to work our way through the building.

One of the happiest days of my life was when I got a job in a factory. What bliss! I promised myself that I'd never be involved in sales again. What I had experienced was abusive to both buyer and seller. Both were sullied.

I actually made it through college, burned all my books, and promised I'd never do *that* again either. After some more adventures, and attempts at trying to find something I *did* want to do, I found myself the director of a residential yoga and meditation community. We arose at 3:30 A.M. each day, took a cold shower, and did two-and-a-half hours of yoga and meditation. I would have been happy doing yoga and meditating all day long. However, part of the lifestyle was to take what you gained from your morning discipline and apply it in the everyday world. Toward that end, many living in the residential community started their own businesses so they could live the values in their daily activities.

I was involved in several small, entrepreneurial ventures. Despite my aversion to going back to school, I decided it would be in my growing enterprises' best interest if I got an MBA; I was fortunate enough to get accepted at Harvard Business School, which was nearby. I could go to school and stay plugged into the businesses.

Following my MBA, I founded a computer systems company. After burning through our venture capital, we came to the moment when the new company actually had to sell something. For me, that was a crisis and a conundrum. On one hand, as an overly responsible type and founder of the company, I felt that if there wasn't enough revenue, it was up to me to bring it in. On the other hand, my experience in sales had led me to believe that you could be either a salesperson or a spiritual person but not both.

Dynamic tension is sometimes the cauldron of creativity. I aggressively sought out any source that would aid my quest for a highly effective yet mutually respectful means of what I used to call selling. The combination was tricky. There were times I felt very honorable—and failed miserably. There were times I was successful in getting immediate revenue—and compromised my values and probably my long-term relationship with the customer. There were times I thought I had it all together—and still fell flat on my face. Yet eventually, everything started to come together. Not only was I successful at that which I'd once feared and hated, it also became what I most enjoyed.

When we eventually sold the computer company, I had the freedom to choose what I wanted to do next. I had been so profoundly and positively impacted by my evolution in sales, I thought others might benefit from what I had learned. I had the good fortune to connect with Bob Elmore, who was the head of Business Systems Consulting at Arthur Andersen (may they rest in peace). After researching global best practices in selling business consulting and technology services and products, I designed and taught a course for Arthur Andersen partners. It was successful and over time became the firm's worldwide model for face-to-face selling.

The success at Andersen led to engagements with other top-notch firms—and to another dilemma. I was looking to have fun, not to build another big business. My wife and I had moved on from the spiritual community and were living on a beautiful, peaceful, eighty-acre property in the mountains above Boulder, Colorado. Neither one of us was eager for me to spend most of my time travelling. Additionally, my goal was to never have more than one employee, and that quickly became impossible. Luckily, one of my clients was FranklinCovey. They valued what I brought to the table enough to purchase my company in 1999. It has been an excellent relationship. They let me do what I'm good at and enjoy while providing global scale, great people, and good management. Our division is called the FranklinCovey Sales Performance Group.

As part of the purchase, I agreed to write a book. The book was to be written in my "spare time" as we were building a new business. I asked how long it took to publish a book and was told the process was about eighteen months from start to finish. That was a problem. Microsoft wanted five thousand copies of this unwritten book for their Worldwide Partner Conference, which was in four months. Knowing what to write was not a problem; I had been living, practicing, and teaching the material for many years. The problem was the time line. We solved that problem by self-publishing the book, called *Let's Get Real or Let's Not Play: The Demise of Dysfunctional Selling and the Advent of Helping Clients Succeed.*

I am proud of that book. Distributed only through FranklinCovey and Amazon.com, it has sold over 100,000 copies. Yet when Penguin approached us with the opportunity to rewrite and significantly expand the book, I was excited. Since the first book was written, my Sales Performance Group colleagues and I have worked with tens of thousands of salespeople and consultants from some of the world's most successful companies. The Helping Clients Succeed coursework has been taught in over forty countries in nine different languages. We have coached and consulted on initiatives involving many billions of dollars of sales. The new book thus benefits from almost a decade of rigorous application, continuous improvement, and entirely new material.

Application, improvement, new material. What a great segue to introducing Randy Illig, since he has been instrumental in all three. When I first met Randy, he was the founder and CEO of a highly successful information technology consulting firm, which was to be awarded Microsoft's Business Solution of the Year. He and his company were looking for sales training and I was the one they interviewed from the Sales Performance Group. After getting a thumbs-up from a couple of his key executives, I met with Randy. We hit it off, he hired us, and I did the training.

Randy, unlike many CEOs, attended the training and immediately put it to practice with clients. He is the type of leader who leads by example, and he sets a great example. After a while, he called me and said, "Okay. This is good stuff. It works. How do we implement it throughout our company? How do we get really good at it? How do we keep improving?" My answer was, "Do more training. We'll reinforce the basics and keep adding more advanced skills." There was a period of silence, followed by his long, drawn-out "Okaaaay." I could hear in his voice the unspoken, "That's it?" We both knew more training would be helpful and yet it was not the complete answer to his questions.

Randy took it upon himself to implement the changes he felt were necessary. His company continued its success and was subsequently sold, freeing Randy to ponder what would be an interesting and challenging use of his time. Fortunately, he contacted me to see if we might be interested in what he could contribute to the Sales Performance Group. Not surprisingly, we were. Randy came on board and immediately led two important efforts. The first was to develop a coaching and consulting practice to allow us to work directly with clients in the field. The second was a sales leadership program to enable clients to leverage and sustain their investment in sales training by turning sales managers into sales leaders. His efforts have paid big dividends for our clients and for FranklinCovey.

Randy has a passionate focus on helping clients succeed. Early in his tenure he felt we needed to improve our ability to help clients with demand generation. While it may be hard to remember, the mid- to late 1990s was largely a time of demand fulfillment. You rowed your boat out into the sea of opportunity and the fish jumped into the boat. Your job was to figure out which fish to keep and to make sure they stayed in the boat.

The fish that were too small were gently released in case they became bigger fish later on. The best fishermen would get the best fish, but there seemed to be plenty of fish for everyone.

Then came the new century and everything changed. Not only were the fish not jumping into the boat, they were hiding and swimming away. Many had been hooked before and were determined to not let it happen again. Bait that had worked before was aggressively rejected. Average fishermen came home empty. Even the best fishermen had to adapt their tactics and improve their skills. They couldn't always wait for the fish to come to them; they had to go find the fish. In our current and more typical sales environment, generating demand is clearly as critical as fulfilling it. Randy led a team effort to build and deploy a demand generation capability that is differentiated by both its approach and the superior results it produces.

The story is unfinished. Though Randy and I are the authors of this book, we are really the spokespeople for numerous colleagues and clients with whom we work. Collectively we keep pushing ourselves to grow, to improve, and to excel. We are utilizing new learning technologies to help salespeople accelerate and magnify their ability to help clients succeed. We are refining and adding to our offerings. We are implementing new business models that give individuals and organizations a variety of means by which to improve their sales performance.

We invite you to join the adventure and add to the ongoing story. This book is our contribution to what we hope will be a continuing dialogue. May it serve you well.

LET'S GET REAL
OR LET'S NOT PLAY

INTRODUCTION

Sales skills are life skills. What makes us better at sales makes us better in life. And vice versa. As we hone our abilities in sales, we learn to think more clearly and communicate more effectively. We use our time, and others' time, more efficiently. We confront and overcome core human fears. We become more alert and flexible. Life is more engaging and enjoyable.

Likewise, almost all fields of study and areas of experience have meaningful application to sales, whether directly or through the use of metaphors and analogies. Insights and learning that profoundly affect our lives can dramatically increase our sales capabilities.

While many, if not most, human endeavors involve selling at some level, this book is geared toward people involved in business-to-business sales. It is intended for those looking to develop ongoing relationships, versus one-time transactions. In ongoing relationships both buyers and sellers must engage in a symbiotic relationship of mutual satisfaction; otherwise someone is going to want out. It is important to make a sale today in a way that will lead to even more sales in the future.

The material in this book is tilted toward the complex sale, in which there are multiple people, multiple interactions, significant investments, and nontrivial business issues. If you are involved in less-complex sales, you will still find the process and skills found on these pages helpful, although you will likely move through them more quickly and in less depth.

Many businesspeople believe that every person and activity in an organization affects sales—one way or another. We agree. This book's natural audience is composed of those professionals directly responsible for topline growth. Nonetheless, it should prove beneficial, whether your connection to sales is full-time or part-time; whether you are already successful or on your way; whether you are experienced or new to the endeavor.

DEFINITION OF TERMS

There are a few terms used throughout the book that warrant some clarification upfront.

Sales: We think of sales as the process of helping clients succeed in a way they feel good about. To us, helping clients succeed is not a euphemism for sales—it is the essence of sales.

> ❖ One thing we've discovered with certainty is that anything we do that makes the customer more successful inevitably results in a financial return for us.   —Jack Welsh

Client: We use this term to mean anyone whom we are trying to help succeed. The client can be either current or potential. The client can be internal or external to an organization. The client can be multiple people, and often is.

For our purposes, client and customer are synonymous. For consistency, we use the term client throughout the book. If, in your world, the term customer is more common, please use that in your mind as you read.

Consultant: We use the term consultant to mean anyone trying to help a client succeed. A consultant can be a salesperson, business developer, advisor, technical or professional consultant, or a friend. Please read into the word "consultant" a meaning that is appropriate for you.

Getting "real": This is a subjective term, used in this book to mean being authentic, being truthful, saying what we mean, being congruent with what we value. Getting real involves challenging lazy thinking and penetrating façades, games, defenses, fears, and illusions. We open belief systems to examination. We get to the heart of the matter.

Exact Solution: No solution is perfect. We get closer and closer, but never get there completely. We use the term "a solution that exactly meets the client's needs" to represent a solution that is not more than the client needs, nor less than what is possible. It is a target rather than an absolute.

It also happens to be the "E" of the OR-DER acronym, which is the key organizing model in the book.

> ❖ It is reasonable to have perfection in our eye that we may always advance toward it, though we know it can never be reached. —*Samuel Johnson*

AWARENESS AND CHOICE

There is no ultimate sales methodology or one right way of doing things. If what you are currently doing is getting you the results you want, keep doing it. This book offers additive options rather than necessary imperatives. Take what you find useful and leave what you do not need. Our goal is to augment your awareness of what is possible to accomplish in sales dialogues, and to increase your choices for succeeding in a way that benefits both you and the client. Increased awareness and greater flexibility translate into greater success and enjoyment.

WHY BOTHER TO READ THIS BOOK?

A tremendous opportunity exists to radically increase the success and satisfaction of both buyers and sellers. There are much more productive ways to find a good fit between what buyers truly need and what solution providers do well. It is worth the effort. With a good fit, both parties win. With a bad fit, both lose.

Unfortunately, many buyers feel that salespeople try to force or coerce a fit. No matter what you put in front of the word "selling" (consultative, solution, visionary, creative, integrity, value-based), it is still tainted with the association of a person doing something *to* somebody, rather than *for* or *with* them. Even talented and ethical sales professionals can be judged guilty until proven innocent.

As it has evolved, the sales relationship has often become a fear-based relationship. Rare is the client who has not felt abused by a salesperson through manipulation, dishonesty, or incompetence. As a result, many clients fear that a salesperson will talk them into something that is not really right for them, that does not meet their needs or create value. They fear they will overpay or be persuaded to make foolish decisions. Poor purchasing decisions can affect their jobs and the fates of many people in their organization. Clients may suspect that salespeople won't really understand their business, that they will be ignorant, arrogant, and elusive. They worry that precious time will be wasted.

Salespeople, on the other hand, may fear they won't make the sale. If they "lose" enough sales, they won't make quota, they won't get paid well, and they won't meet their own needs or those of the people important to them. Salespeople have also learned that many requests for their involvement are not sincere, that the client has no intention of hiring them. Perhaps the client wants to check out prices and see what is happening in the marketplace. Perhaps the client has already decided who they are going to hire, but they are required to have three additional bids. Some clients have no qualms whatsoever in having solution providers invest huge amounts of time, people, and money with no real expectation of having a working relationship.

Dysfunctional buying practices have arisen to combat dysfunctional selling practices. For instance, buyers may send out Requests for Proposals (RFPs) that, under threat of pain and death, refuse to allow any human being to talk to any other human being. When buyers do not trust sellers, they hide and protect vital information and restrict personal contact. Sellers have to guess what would actually work for the client, and often guess wrong. This reinforces the perception that sellers can't be trusted, and dissatisfied buyers then create even higher hurdles. Sellers acquiesce and either go along with things that do not make sense, try more outlandish gambits, or choose to withdraw.

Buyers hate having their time wasted yet are all too willing to waste sellers' time. Sellers are asked to fill out pages of questions, whether they seem relevant or not. Sellers are asked to make large, up-front investments of time and energy, and to reveal proprietary knowledge with no reciprocity from the buyer. Buyers' current problems have been developing over years, yet they want sellers to propose a solution in two weeks. Some clients have concluded that they do not have to pay for services. They put out an RFP to five or six companies; they have each one explain at length what they would do and how they would do it; they then take the best of what they heard and do it themselves. Presto—free consulting!

Buyers express the desire for "fairness," a "level playing field," and the ability "to compare apples to apples." Yet, in requiring formulaic responses to the RFP, buyers may unwittingly enforce a conformity that results in sterility and a lack of creativity and innovation, and which eliminates potentially good alternatives. Buyers may ask sellers to agree to one-sided, onerous terms and conditions as a prerequisite for merely responding to the RFP. Excellent solution providers may even choose not to respond. It can eliminate intelligent and creative negotiation that could serve both parties.

So again, why bother to read this book? Because collectively we can make a difference. We can replace dysfunctional *selling* practices with attitudes, skills, and processes focused on helping clients succeed. We can transform dysfunctional *buying* practices into those that serve clients more appropriately. We can promote an environment where buyers and sellers talk honestly and openly, then jointly make intelligent decisions about whether or not it makes sense to work together. If it does *not* make sense, let's find out quickly, shake hands, and part friends. If it *does* make sense, let's have some fun, do good things, and make some money.

SAYS WHO?

While grounded in research, this book emanates from the authors' direct experience. We both are responsible for initiating and developing accounts with multiple Fortune 500 companies. We coach and consult with clients in the field. Along with our colleagues, we have positively influenced billions of dollars of sales; we benefit from a great number of repetitions in a field where success, or the lack thereof, is unmistakable. Both of us have held CEO and other leadership positions, providing perspective beyond the sales arena.

"If you want to learn something, teach it." The content of this book has been taught to demanding audiences in over forty countries and in nine different languages. We do what we teach and teach what we do. When something works, makes sense, and is consistent with core values, we apply it. If it continues to work, we reinforce, repeat, and reward. If it does not work, we rip apart, reevaluate, and replace. What is in this book has been thoroughly tested and has served both buyers and sellers extremely well.

HOW THIS BOOK IS ORGANIZED

There are four major sections in the book. "Key Beliefs" lays out underlying premises upon which the rest of the book's content is based. The next sections are "Qualifying," "Winning," and "Initiating." Initiating is placed *last* in this book even though it may come *first* in a sales cycle. This placement is for learning purposes; when you reach the Initiating section, you will have all the skills and abilities described in Qualifying and Winning, thus allowing you to initiate effectively. Initiating new opportunities with strangers is challenging; the task is easier when a broad array of choices is available.

The following provides a quick sense of what each of these three sections entails.

Qualifying: Should we keep talking?
How do both we and the client make intelligent decisions about
    whether or not to invest energy and resources in an opportunity?
Winning: Should you do this with us?
How do we effectively advocate for a solution that precisely meets the
    clients' needs? How do we enable good decisions in the client's best
    interests?
Initiating: Should we be talking?
How do we develop opportunities from scratch, in a way that both we
    and the client can feel good about?

This book is an overview, not an encyclopedia. In every single aspect, a deeper experience is available. While some exercises for acquiring and applying skills are included, this book is not a substitute for a training course; training courses are not a substitute for working together in the field. If the overview here resonates and you want to explore further, give the authors a call. It's a good way to see if we walk our talk.

CHAPTER ONE

KEY BELIEFS

Every sales or decision-making methodology has underlying assumptions and beliefs. Sometimes they are clearly stated and sometimes they are not. We base our methodology on the following premises:

1. Consultants and clients want the same thing.
2. Intent counts more than technique (and technique is still important). *Corollary:* You are more successful when you concentrate on the success of others rather than on your own.
3. Solutions have no inherent value.
4. Methodology matters.
5. World-class inquiry precedes world-class advocacy.

KEY BELIEF NO. 1:
Consultants and Clients Want the Same Thing

There is a level at which consultants and clients share identical, mutual self-interests. Both want a solution that exactly meets the clients' needs. If clients do not perceive they are getting a solution that meets their needs, they can choose to do nothing or go somewhere else. If enough clients make either choice, consultants start hurting.

It can be even worse for you if clients *do* buy your solution and *then* discover that it does not meet their needs. In that case, you can spend all of your profits (sometimes more) trying to make it right. If you can't make it right, you have an unhappy, nonreferenceable client. Sometimes you spend the effort and money to make it right and still end up with a dissatisfied and disenchanted client. Furthermore, the Internet makes it easy for buyers to widely broadcast their experiences—whether positive or negative. The authors have worked with companies that have lost hundreds of millions of dollars on sales they wish they had never made. Consultants clearly lose when clients think they are not getting a solution that truly meets their needs.

Clients lose as well. If they do not buy a solution, all the problems they were hoping to resolve go unsolved. All the results they hoped to achieve are not attained. If they do buy a solution and it does not meet their needs, they waste a great amount of money and time in the solution-acquisition and implementation processes, and still forgo the expected economic benefits. With each additional attempt to create a solution, both consultants and client sponsors are met with exponentially more cynicism and resistance, and less likelihood of success.

Buyers and sellers both want a solution that meets the client's needs exactly. We both win if we get it; we both lose if we do not. That is the good news; knowing we both want the same thing makes the task easier.

The bad news is that clients do not consistently get a solution that meets their needs. Even though both of us want it, even though we both lose if it does not happen, we both often engage in counterproductive behaviors. Let's increase our awareness of those behaviors as a prelude to building better choices.

Dysfunctional Behaviors of Consultants

When we ask consultants what *they* do that inhibits arriving at a solution that completely meets the client's needs, here are some of the things they tell us:

"We don't listen."
"We make assumptions."

"We don't talk to the right people."

"We think we know what they need better than they do."

"We try to fit their needs into our solution."

"We need to make the sale."

"It takes too much time."

"We don't understand their business."

Dysfunctional Behaviors of Clients

What about the clients? They want a solution that meets their needs, yet they also exhibit counterproductive behaviors and actions that get in the way. Common consultant complaints about clients include:

"They don't know what they need."

"They can't articulate what they need."

"They don't agree on what they need."

"They won't give us good information."

"They don't let us talk to the right people."

"They are unrealistic about the time, money, and people needed."

"Politics and personal issues count more than business sense."

"They procrastinate."

"They won't make decisions."

If we keep focusing on a solution that exactly meets the client's needs, it will organize and guide our behaviors toward a common goal. It becomes a touchstone against which we can test all requested actions. Whenever we request something of the client, or they ask something of us, we examine whether that effort will take us closer to, rather than farther from, a solution that exactly meets the client's needs.

Concentrating on common interests—what we both want—does not eliminate the possibility that we and the client will have interests that differ, or even conflict. For instance, when it comes to creating value for the client—making the pie bigger—we and the client want the same thing: a bigger pie. When deciding how much to *pay* for the increased value (dividing up the pie), our self-interests may diverge; each party may feel they deserve more of the pie. Most people find that making the pie bigger makes it much easier to negotiate a meaningful slice. If we do not have a solution that meets the client's needs, there may be no pie to divide.

KEY BELIEF NO. 2:
Intent Counts More Than Technique
(and Technique Is Still Important)

If you are going to help your clients succeed, you will need good information from them. To get that information, you will ask questions. Your clients will decide how much information to disclose based largely on their perception of the intent behind your questions: Are you asking questions to help *them* get what *they* want in a way *they* feel good about, or to help *you* get what *you* want in a way *you* feel good about? If they give you information, can they trust that you will use it *for* their interests and not *against* them? Many clients make these judgments instinctively, at a subconscious level. Nonetheless, you can influence those judgments.

> ❖ Who you are stands over you and thunders so I cannot hear what you say.   —*Emerson*

There is an old maxim: "People don't care how much you know, until they know how much you care."

Building Trust

In his book *The Speed of Trust*, our friend and former colleague Stephen M. R. Covey details and demonstrates two key points:

   1. The degree of trust has hard economic consequences: as trust goes up, speed goes up and costs go down. As trust decreases, everything slows and costs rise. (Most of us understand this intuitively; Stephen backs it up with evidence.)

   2. You can build trust on purpose. Earning trust is a skill that you can learn and improve. It need not be left to good luck, circumstance, or hope.

We describe trust as follows: Trust = Intent + Expertise. Clients must trust that your intent is compatible with their best interests, and that you have the expertise to design and deliver a solution that meets their needs. For most consultants, how you can increase your expertise is far more clear than how you can improve clients' perception of your intent. Yet if clients do not feel comfortable with your intent, they may discount your expertise.

A client will assign to you an intent whether you want them to or not. The intent they assign to you will have a large impact on the quality of your dialogue. If your intent is not crystal clear to you, it will not be clear to the client.

We highly recommend that you write out an Intent Statement and develop the ability to act congruently with that intent, even under pressure. A good exercise for clarifying intent is provided in Appendix Two.

Corollary: You Are More Successful When You Concentrate on the Success of Others Rather Than on Your Own.

When people feel they are being manipulated or led to *your* conclusion rather than to their own, they will often move aggressively in the opposite direction. This behavior is called reactance, or polarity response. The irony with reactance is that the harder you try to "sell" people, the less likely it is to happen. People feel their choice is being restricted and they become highly motivated to subvert the limitation. It is an emotional response.

> ❖ The intention behind an action determines its effects, every intention affects both us and others, and the effects of intents extend far beyond the physical world. . . . It is, therefore, wise for us to become aware of the many intentions that inform our experience to sort out which intentions produce which effects, and to choose our intention according to the effects that we desire to produce.
> —*Gary Zukav, The Seat of the Soul*

When trust is compromised, information flow is severely curtailed, and you are far less likely to craft a solution they feel meets their needs. Conversely, when clients perceive that your intent is to help them succeed, they are more likely to share their beliefs about what that success is. The better you understand what the client wants and needs, the better the choices you can bring to the table. It is in your own best interest to focus on the interest of the client first.

> ❖ The moment there is suspicion about a person's motives, everything he does becomes tainted.
> —Mahatma Gandhi

Some part of us understands this dynamic. Yet we often feel pressured to meet our personal and organizational revenue goals. Our intent becomes "Meet the goals! Make the sale!" Perversely, the harder we try, the worse we do. When we lose sight of helping our clients succeed and instead focus on our own success, clients perceive the difference negatively. Please remember: *The more important it is to meet* your *numbers, the more important it is to stop concentrating on* your *numbers and start concentrating on the* clients' *numbers.*

We are more successful when we concentrate on the success of others rather than on our own. This is not a platitude. It is something the authors know from experience. We have sold to survive ("I've got to get some sales"), we have sold out of ego ("I can get them to do this"), and we have helped clients succeed. We know the difference in our hearts, minds, and guts. Helping clients succeed not only feels better, it is tremendously more effective.

> ❖ The more important it is to meet your numbers, the more important it is to stop concentrating on your numbers and start concentrating on the client's numbers.

Helping clients succeed is not an attempt to be nice; it is not philanthropic or selfless. It is a powerful, if paradoxical, means of getting what we want.

Technique Is Still Important

Clearly, technique is important. You could be the most well-intentioned person in the world, a fine human being, yet if you have no communication skills—no critical-thinking tools—you will not be successful. A good portion of this book deals with technique. If that technique does not serve your intent, and if that intent does not serve the people you are working with, everything else will be jeopardized.

KEY BELIEF NO. 3:
Solutions Have No Inherent Value

Consultants often deal in foregone solutions. We tend to think everyone needs what we have, that our solution has universal application. However, solutions derive value only from the problems they solve *that people care about,* and/or from producing results *that people highly value.* Solutions must solve something. If there is nothing the client wants to solve, there is no value to the proposed solution. Understanding this axiom guides everything we do with clients.

Consultants are often eager to tell their clients, "The solution to your problem is . . ." Let's take a moment and examine that short phrase. Before reading further, take a couple of minutes and write down the assumptions contained in the phrase:

"The solution to the problem is . . ."

Did you come up with some of the following assumptions?

- The problem is real; it exists; it has not gone away or was not an illusion. Likewise, a solution exists that solves the problem.
- There is only one problem. There are not multiple problems or several different problems intertwined. Likewise, there is only one solution.
- People care about the problem; they want a solution.
- The problem is a priority relative to other problems.
- We can measure the extent of the problem.
- It is possible to determine if the solution is valid.
- Different people perceive the problem the same way.
- The solution would solve the entire problem.
- The cost of the solution is meaningfully less than the cost of the problem.
- The solution would not cause more problems, or a worse problem.

- The solution will be valid over time.
- The solution can adapt to changing circumstances.
- The solution can and will be applied to the problem.
- Someone is willing and able to allocate sufficient resources to address the problem.

You could do the same exercise, with similar conclusions, using the phrase, "The solution to the opportunity is . . ."

> ❖ Solutions have to solve problems that people care about or produce results people highly value.

How you sell is a free sample of how you solve. It does not demonstrate good critical thinking skills if you are willing to talk about a solution without examining some of the assumptions listed earlier. Yet consultants do so a large percentage of the time. When you start talking about a solution before understanding what it is supposed to solve, you decrease client confidence, lessen your credibility, and significantly reduce your ability to produce an exact solution.

A Mutual Conspiracy

There is a mutual conspiracy between client and consultant to talk about the solution early on. We love talking about the solution. It is our comfort zone. We understand it, we know it, it's about us, it's our solution, and it's really great. What about clients? They like to believe there is a magic formula—that they can throw some money at the situation and everything will be okay. It is easier to talk about a solution than to do the critical spadework to uncover the issues the solution is supposed to resolve; to find evidence that proves they have a problem; to develop measurements for success; to explore systemic implications; to identify and overcome constraints. In addition, as long as the solution is the topic of discussion, clients can put all the pressure on you; they can sit back and watch you sing and dance.

Move Off the Solution

Top professionals have the ability to "move off the solution." They withhold offering a solution until they have intelligently explored the problems to be solved and/or the results to be achieved. They organize their questioning to get meaningful answers to critical assumptions. They do so in a way that is comfortable, conversational, and time-efficient. When done well, clients gain insight and understanding of their situation.

In the section entitled Initiating, we discuss how to move off our *own* solution, and in the Qualifying section, we talk about how to move off the solution the *client* proposes. Because of the "mutual conspiracy" to talk about the solution, moving off the solution requires that consultants exercise considerable discipline and communication skill.

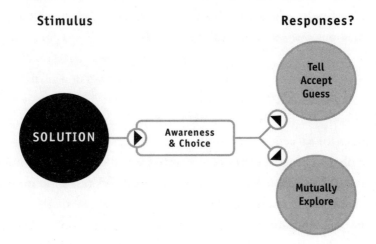

The Big Marshmallow

In his book *Emotional Intelligence*, Dr. Daniel Goleman refers to a remarkable study conducted by Walter Mischel during the 1960s at a preschool on the campus of Stanford University. He took children who were about four years old and put them in a room alone with a marshmallow on the table. The researcher would tell the child he or she could have the marshmallow, but if the child could wait while the researcher ran a quick errand, he would bring back two marshmallows. For a child, that is a pretty good return on investment.

The researcher would then leave the room; the child was surreptitiously filmed. Some of the kids had no restraint. The idea of waiting to eat that marshmallow was way beyond them; they grabbed the marshmallow and ate it. Some of them nibbled the marshmallow, taking a tiny bite, then another, and pretty soon the whole marshmallow was gone. Some of them would agonize as they walked around the room, staring at the marshmallow, sniffing it, even licking it, but they would not eat it. Some even tried taking naps to avoid the dilemma.

The researchers then followed these children over a fifteen-year period. The kids who had the patience and discipline to not eat the marshmallow when they were in preschool were more successful emotionally and intellectually, regardless of their chosen pursuits.

Similar results occur with business developers and consultants. The client may put one requested solution on the table. If the consultant can

> ❖ Move off the solution!

resist the impulse to talk about that solution (the adult version of the marshmallow) and instead ask effective questions that investigate what the solution is meant to solve, he or she is often rewarded with multiple opportunities for success.

One of the hardest behaviors to overcome is the tendency to immediately go for the first solution. Consultants who can resist the immediate solution are more successful.

Move off the solution!

KEY BELIEF NO. 4:
Methodology Matters

There is no one way to help clients succeed.

There are, however, critical thinking skills which greatly aid our diagnosis of and prescription for business challenges. We refer to these skills and principles collectively as the business intelligence quotient (IQ^B or, simply, IQ). How intelligently can we uncover where and how value is created in an application, function, process, unit, organization, or economy? How critically can we examine our beliefs? How much intellectual rigor can we apply to our analysis? Good IQ helps us clarify and test our assumptions and mental models, balance our gut instinct with data, gather evidence and impact for key issues, confront critical constraints (past, present, and future), and apply good tenets of systemic thinking.

There are communication and relationship skills that significantly enhance the quality of client/consultant interactions; we refer to those skills as principles of emotional quotient (EQ). How well can we create a container of safety and trust, where clients feel free to share what they think, feel, and believe to be true? How comfortable do clients feel with us examining and exploring their beliefs? How much information will they share? How willing are they to give us access to key stakeholders?

Finally, there are process and execution skills that save time, increase productivity, leverage resources, and eliminate non–value added effort; we refer to these as execution quotient (XQ). Can we execute a consistent, repeatable, flexible process that works better for both clients and consultants? Can we build feedback loops into the process which allow us to continually improve?

For top-performing consultants it is the *fusion* of these skill sets that puts them at the pinnacle of their profession. They seamlessly blend IQ, EQ, and XQ.

Intellectual Piranha Versus Warm and Fuzzy

Mahan once interacted with one of the world's top strategy consulting firms. Their consultants would eat, drink, and sleep IQ. Some of their own clients described them as "brains on a stick." In their meetings, when they would throw an idea on the table, it was like watching piranhas feed. They would attack and devour the idea, tear it apart, and if anything was left at the end they would say, "Oh, must be a good idea." For them it was a valid form of critical thinking. The problem was that when they tried to use the "piranha process" with their clients, their clients found it tremendously arrogant and obnoxious—and probably intimidating. What worked well as an internal paradigm transferred poorly to external situations; there was little flexibility to adapt styles to differing requirements. This inflexibility proved a serious challenge as the firm decided to make implementation a major plank of their own strategy. Clients would put up with them for two or three weeks, maybe even for two or three months, but rarely for two or three years. They had to significantly stretch their EQ to help their clients (and themselves) succeed.

We've also worked with companies that were much higher in EQ than IQ. One company in particular had an incredible ability to develop rapport and trust with clients, and they backed that ability with quality content; yet they lacked the intellectual horsepower to really connect their services to business results. This was a serious limitation in helping clients succeed and thus impeded their growth potential. To truly help clients succeed, both IQ and EQ are necessary. Lack of either is a fatal flaw.

It is helpful to organize these skills into a repeatable methodology (an XQ) that makes explicit our beliefs about the IQ and EQ abilities that are most effective in increasing profitable revenue. Those beliefs can then be tested in the "real world." With the appropriate data and anecdotal feedback, we can assess the following:

Is what we are doing producing the results we want?
If so, reinforce, repeat, reward, and improve.
If not, is it because

- we are not actually applying the methodology? (Increase application.)

- we are not applying the methodology skillfully? (Increase skill.)
- the methodology is faulty? (Rip apart, reevaluate, and replace.)

The ORDER Methodology

Methodologies can help us take a complex (sometimes even chaotic) series of events and processes and represent them in an understandable, repeatable, and transferable way. They can help integrate sophistication with simplicity. If it is too sophisticated it will not be used, and if it is too simple it will not make a difference. Many business development methodologies tend to emphasize completeness and thoroughness over ease of adoption and application. They are very good but rarely used, and thus are not as helpful as they could be.

The ORDER methodology is an abstract of how people develop business at a high level of expertise. The "what" of the model—its fundamental premise—stays consistent throughout the global economy. The "how"— the way in which people apply it—changes considerably among countries, cultures, cities, industries, solutions, and personalities.

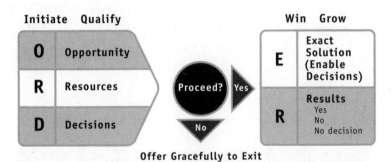

Following is a brief overview of the ORDER methodology and its key components. The rest of this book examines each component in detail.

Opportunity: Should *they do it?*

You cannot help someone succeed who has no perceived needs or wants. No pain, no gain, no opportunity. You can develop a mutual understanding of an opportunity by examining the following:

Issues: What problems or results is the client trying to address? In what priority?

Evidence: How do we define the problem? How do we measure success?

Impact: What are the financial and intangible costs and benefits?

Context: Who or what else is affected by the issues and the solution?

Constraints: What has stopped (or might stop) the organization from resolving these issues?

Resources: Can they do it?

Even if there is a substantial opportunity, you cannot help someone succeed who has insufficient resources. You must examine:

Time: When are they hoping to see the results in place?

People: Which people resources are they willing to commit?

Money: What level of investment is appropriate for the desired results?

Decisions: How will the decision be made, and by whom?

Even if there is a substantial Opportunity with sufficient available Resources, you cannot help someone succeed who cannot or will not make a decision.

To understand and influence how decisions will be made, it is helpful to codevelop the following with the client:

The Decision Process

Steps	Decision	When	Who	Criteria/ Beliefs
What are all of the steps?	What decision gets made in each step?	When will they decide?	Who is involved in each step	How will each decision maker decide?

Competition:	How will they decide between alternative solutions?
Gain/Loss:	Who in the organization stands to win or lose if this solution is adopted?
Personal Stake:	How does the person we are talking with win or lose?

Exact Solution / Enable Decisions: Will they do it with us?
- What is our solution? Given the client's situation, what are the reasons that adopting our solution makes sense?
- How can we effectively advocate for our solution and enable good decisions?

Results: Will they do more with us?

In response to our presentation, our client will say yes, no, or make no decision. For each of those responses there are actions that are helpful to ensure a positive and productive ongoing relationship.

Yes: How do we deliver and measure the desired results? How do we build and grow a value based relationship?

No: How do we learn and improve through understanding where our solution did not meet the client's needs better than other options?

No decision: How do we co-develop a means for the client to feel comfortable making an explicit, concrete decision—either Yes or No?

ORDER is depicted in a linear fashion. In practice it is applied in an iterative way. The information that comes from ORD is often developed over many conversations, like fitting pieces into a puzzle over time. Even though there is a logical progression of ORD before ER, elements of ER will enter into our ORD discussions.

The better the job we do with ORD, the higher the probability of success in ER. If there is not a qualified opportunity, with sufficient available resources, and if there is not a clearly defined decision process with access to the people we need to see, then neither our client, nor we, have earned the solution.

Some competencies, skill sets, and mental models for ORD are different than those for ER:

Opportunity—Resources— Decisions	Exact Solution / Enabling Decisions—Results
• *Divergent thinking:* developing multiple issues; considering many possibilities; talking to many people; systemic thinking	• *Convergent thinking:* driving to a decision; resolving issues and concerns; implementation; measurement; continuous improvement
• *Inquiry:* seeking first to understand	• *Advocacy:* seeking to be understood
• Understanding *effects* of problems	• Understanding *causes* of problems
• *Deciding* fit	• *Executing* fit

Evolution of ORDER Over the Sales Cycle

Initiating: Should we be talking? (Filling the pipeline)

When we initiate a dialogue with a prospective client, we prepare both to *Ask* and to *Offer.*

- *Ask:* A process of inquiry to allow the client to set the agenda.
- *Offer:* Some reasons we feel it would make sense for the client to invest time speaking with us. Those reasons are based on a set of educated guesses about a potential Opportunity, which indicate a potential relevance of our solution(s) to the client's situation.

Qualifying: Should we keep talking? (Advancing the pipeline)

We are in the qualifying phase when:

- a client initiates the conversation, or
- a client reacts with interest to something we initiate.

We qualify by talking about Opportunity, Resources, Decisions, and testing possible elements of an Exact Solution.

Roadmap	Initiate	Qualify	Win
Opportunity			
Issues			
Evidence			
Impact			
Context			
Constraints			
Resources			
Time			
People			
Money			
Decisions			
Process			
Access			
Criteria/Beliefs			
Alternatives			
Exact Solution			
Solution			
Deal Structure			
Enabling Decisions			
End in Mind			
Key Beliefs			
Proof/Action			
Questions			
Yellow Lights			
Next Steps			
Results			
Yes			
No			
No Decision			
Relationships			
Who			
How			

Winning (Delivering the pipeline)
    Our proposed solution should be able to:

- enable the Opportunity
- utilize the available Resources
- match the Decision Criteria/Beliefs of key stakeholders
- exceed their alternatives

For those who like to get the big picture before diving into the details, there is a roadmap to "Helping Clients Succeed" on page 23.

KEY BELIEF NO. 5:
World-Class Inquiry Precedes World-Class Advocacy

Successful business development is a balance between inquiry and advocacy. Stephen Covey's sixth habit of highly successful people, "Seek first to understand—then to be understood," applies to highly successful business developers. Skilled inquiry produces *mutual* understanding: we better understand what the client truly values; the client gains better clarity of his/her own situation and possibilities; the client *feels* understood. The better job we do of eliciting the client's story, the more able we are to match it to ours.

> ❖ The only way to influence someone is to find out what they want and show them how to get it. —*Dale Carnegie*

Most people know how to ask questions and hear what others are saying, yet few are consciously competent at developing a high degree of mutual understanding. They lack either a powerful methodology of questioning, the ability to truly listen with all their senses, or both, often while thinking that this is surely not the case.

Consultants commonly resort to three traditional approaches to interacting with clients:

1. We Tell.

When inquiry and advocacy are out of balance, the tilt is almost always toward advocacy. "Telling" is not always bad. Sometimes trusted business advisors help their clients cut through fear, uncertainty, and doubt by strongly advocating what the client must do. We always have telling as a choice. Telling, however, has a low probability of producing a solution that clients feel exactly meets their needs.

The downside of tilting toward advocacy includes:

- What we choose to tell is not interesting or relevant to clients. We waste their time and ours, and reduce the desire for more interaction.
- What we tell them to do might be wrong. (It is at least a statistical possibility.)
- There may be no buy-in or ownership from the client, which could cause failure of either the sale or the initiative.
- They see us as arrogant, ignorant, or both.
- We potentially leave huge amounts of money on the table by telling about one opportunity when asking could have produced many more.
- We lose the ability to match our story to the clients', to speak their language, to address their priorities, to foresee and counteract pitfalls early, and to build trust through understanding.

2. We Accept.

Clients tell us what they want, and we propose to give it to them. Easy, isn't it? Obviously, accepting what clients want is not always bad, particularly if we agree with them. Yet how often do we propose a solution based on what the client said he wanted, and the client either feels it misses the mark, chooses to do nothing, or chooses a competitor whose solution is different than what he asked for? How many times have we won the engagement, given clients what they said they wanted, and still ended up with an unhappy client?

The downside of passively accepting includes:

- The client could be wrong—and will still blame us—sometimes with severe consequences.
- We have not demonstrated any thought leadership.
- We may not understand exactly what we are solving or how to measure success.
- We could leave many opportunities uncovered.

3. We Guess.

Of course, we consultants do not like to call it guessing—we call it diagnosis, assessment, analysis. Yet, if one didn't know better, it would look a lot like guessing. One or two consultants talk to one or two client counterparts for an hour or two. Based on that, they start guessing: What do we think they really need? What do we think the actual problems are? Why haven't they fixed this before now? What should we propose? Do you think we were talking to the right people? Do you think they have any money to pay for this? How much should we charge? Who do you think the competition is? And so on.

Consultants, being the intelligent people we are, have formalized the guessing process; we call it a proposal. And you can always tell how much we are guessing: the more we guess, the longer the proposal. As the cost of face-to-face business development keeps climbing, the cost of guessing becomes enormous.

A Fourth Approach: Mutual Exploration

There is a fourth option: we mutually explore with clients a solution that truly meets their needs—whether they eventually get that solution with us or with someone else. Of course, this is not easy. Clients have come to expect that we will tell, accept, and guess. Even worse, they may try to force us to tell ("You're the expert"), accept ("Just give us what we want"), or guess ("It's all in the RFP").

Mutual exploration has two imagined downsides. First, it would appear to take more time. However, the authors assert that mutual exploration does not take *more* time; it just uses time differently, and more effectively.

Do we *tell*, do we *accept*, do we *guess*, or do we *mutually explore*?

If we do not have a solution that meets the client's needs, it is more time-effective (and cost-effective) to find that out early rather than late. Which leads to the second imagined downside: that we may find we do not have a solution that truly meets the client's needs, and thus "lose" a sale. Yet we cannot lose something we never had; the probability of selling them something if it does not meet their needs is low. Even if they do buy it and only afterward are displeased, we still "lose." Thus, the authors contend we can get the upsides of mutual exploration while turning the perceived downsides into advantages.

What TOP Professionals Do That Others Don't

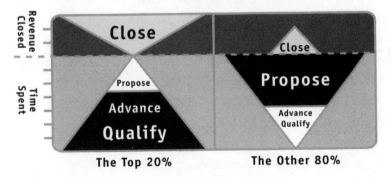

Don't present to open, present to close!

This book is dedicated to mutual exploration and to the goal of a solution that truly meets the client's needs. It may not happen every time, but it definitely can happen far more often than it does now.

CHAPTER TWO

QUALIFYING: OVERVIEW

Qualification is a process of mutual exploration and, we hope, mutual understanding. Both we and the client are making decisions about good fit and about a solution that will precisely meet the client's needs. Mutual exploration takes more time at the beginning of the relationship. It is critical that we use that time to make wise decisions about whether to proceed or to not proceed. "Not a good fit" is a great conclusion, if arrived at early. It is a horrible miscalculation if arrived at late. Poor qualification results in lost sales and markedly drives up business development costs. Extracting energy and resources from low-probability opportunities and investing them in high-probability opportunities is critical to our individual and organizational success.

We are in the qualifying phase when:

- a client initiates the conversation
- a client reacts with interest to something we initiate (see chapter 7).

On what basis should we qualify? The authors, along with our colleagues and clients, have established that the flow of meaningful information between consultant and client is a powerful predictor of success and is critically related to the building of trust and value.

Three factors tend to move together: value, trust, and the flow of meaningful information.

When there is a high degree of trust and an ample flow of meaningful information, we are more likely to produce a solution of value. When we have a credible record of producing value, clients trust us and we are more likely to gain good information. Conversely, when there is little trust or exchange of meaningful information, we are forced to guess about what is actually important to the client and are therefore less likely to develop a solution that is either accepted or produces optimal value. When we do not produce value, trust goes down and subsequent interactions suffer.

Value is a lagging indicator; we find out only afterward if it is realized. Trust is hard to measure. What we can measure is the flow of meaningful information. Over time we can develop a correlation between information received and results achieved. Little or poor-quality information indicates low probability of success. We should use all of our skills to correct the deficiencies or we should gracefully exit the opportunity. We should invest that time in opportunities where the flow of meaningful information is high and where the information indicates good fit.

Of course, low probability does not mean *no* probability. And there's the rub. You could "win" some opportunities even with poor probability indicators. The military maxim "He who defends everything, defends nothing" also applies to business development. To use a different analogy, we have only so many "chips" (time, people, money, energy) to play with, and if we keep betting on low-probability outcomes, we will soon, even with sporadic wins, get cleaned out.

> ❖ Dialogue: "dia" is flow and "logos" is meaning. Dialogue is the free flow of meaning.
>
> ❖ The free flow of meaningful information (the quality of our dialogues) is a strong predictor of sales success.

One of Mahan's clients was in the habit of responding to unsolicited RFPs. They received an RFP and without any conversation whatsoever completed and returned their response. Mahan predicted that since the flow of meaningful information was paltry, this client's win rate was probably low and the costs high. The client decided

> ❖ He who defends everything, defends nothing. —*Military maxim*

to do a study to find out. They reviewed forty-six such RFP responses over an eighteen-month period. While highly variable, the average direct cost to respond was about $80,000 per RFP. The win rate on their responses was *zero*. Thank goodness! If they had won even *one* of those deals, everyone would remember it: "Hey—we won the XYZ account and that was from an unsolicited RFP."

Let's suppose they won that one XYZ account. The associated business development cost would be 46 proposals times $80,000 for a total of $3,680,000. If the profit margin on XYZ would have greatly exceeded that cost, all would be good. However, that was not even close to the reality.

The company instituted a new rule: nobody could respond to RFPs unless they were permitted to talk with at least one human being who was intimately familiar with the the business issues the RFP solutions were meant to address. Like all good rules, that rule was sometimes broken, yet it served this company well.

Another client engaged us to do a "pipeline scrub" on several billion dollars of opportunities; they wanted to do a better job of deciding which deals to invest in and which deals to let go. There were about four hundred deals and the business leader knew that if they approached them all equally, it would be a disaster. He wanted to pursue a maximum of two hundred deals, yet no consultant volunteered to give up half of their potential opportunities. The business leader agreed to use the flow of meaningful information as the primary qualification tool.

We interviewed their consultants about the information they had collected on Opportunity, Resources, and Decisions. It quickly became apparent that many consultants felt deals were qualified based on their own opinions rather than on what their client had actually said. Many times consultants would be emphatic that the client had urgent problems or opportunities. Yet, when we asked them if the client had actually uttered specific words of confirmation about the importance of the challenge, the evidence of its existence, and its impact on the organization, they would say, "No, not exactly." When we asked them how the client would measure success, they were not sure. When we inquired as to what had stopped the client from fixing the problem itself, the consultants had their own guesses and no client opinions. Often, they had not discussed the client's views on time, people, and money. Decision processes were unclear or unfavorable. They did not have access to key stakeholders and thus could not describe what criteria those people would use to make the decision. Based on the flow of meaningful information, these opportunities were not qualified.

It's not a problem or an opportunity until the client says it is. A deal is not qualified because we *think* it is; it is qualified because of what the client says.

> ❖ It is not a problem until the client says it is.

NO GUESSING

If our intent is to help clients succeed, we have both the right and the obligation not to guess about the key elements of that success. Getting real is partly defined by our ability to stop guessing and find out what is really going on.

> ❖ No guessing!

Opportunity: Let's not guess what problems clients are trying to solve and/or what results they want to achieve. Let's not guess about how those problems are defined and how we would recognize when the results are achieved. Let's not guess about the financial and intangible impact of the problems and results. Let's not guess about who or what else is affected by the current situation and the proposed solution. Let's not guess about what has stopped the organization from resolving these challenges before now.

Resources: Let's not guess about when clients need the results in place, about what kind of people-resources they are willing to commit and about how much money they are willing to invest to get the results they want.

Decisions: Let's not guess about the steps they need to take to make a well-informed decision. Let's not guess about what decisions get made in each step, who is involved in making them, and when those decisions will happen. Finally, let's not guess about what criteria they will use to make the decision and the issues they want addressed in order to feel comfortable and confident about the decision they make.

Just Because We Speak the Same Language . . .

Much of the guessing we do involves our interpretation of what people mean by the words they use. Language is imprecise. The following story is an example of language's murkiness:

A woman seeking a divorce went to visit her attorney. The first question he asked her was, "Do you have grounds?" She replied, "Yes, about two acres." He said, "Perhaps I'm not making myself clear. Do you have a grudge?" She responded, "No, but we have a carport." Impatiently, he went on, "Does your husband beat you up?" She smiled and said, "No, I generally get up before him."

> ❖ The greatest enemy of communication is the illusion of it.
> —*Pierre Martineau*

The attorney switched approaches in one last effort, "Ma'am, are you sure you really want a divorce?" She said firmly, "I don't want one at all, but my husband does. He claims we have difficulty communicating."

Words Mean Different Things to Different People

We often mistake fluency (in which we both use the words easily) with comprehension (when we both have the same meanings for the words). We assume that because we know what something means to us, it means the same to everyone else. We assume that other people know what they mean by the words they use, when it is possible that neither of us has a clue.

Clients often describe their situations with what linguists call "complex equivalents" or "high-level abstractions." These are words or phrases that encode many experiences and beliefs into one small package. Like an iceberg, the word floats above the surface and the multiple meanings and interpretations remain hidden below.

The authors and their colleagues have engaged in a "No Guessing"

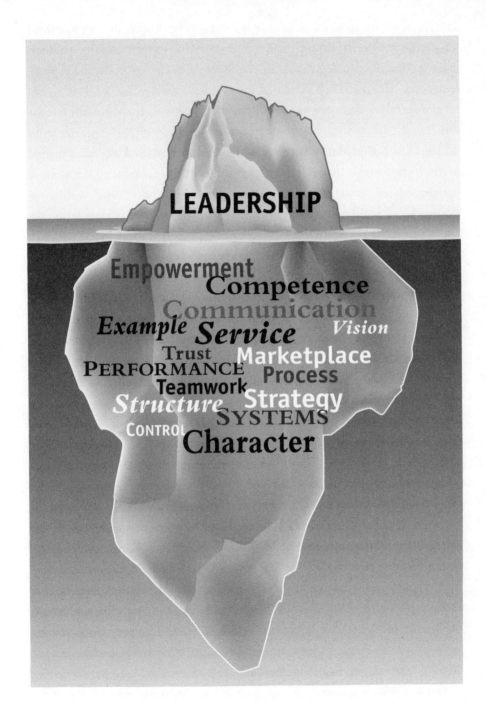

exercise with consultants. In groups of four or five people, they pick a word or phrase that is common in their business such as leadership, strategy, time management, supply chain management, executive compensation, e-procurement, etc. Each person in the group writes down at least ten words or phrases that mean the same thing to him or her as the word chosen for the exercise. They all then estimate how many words will be common to all of the lists. For instance, if the word was education, and one person had written the word "school," how many others in the group would also have written school (or schools)? The words "university" or "college" would not count. Most groups estimate an average of three or four common words, with individual estimates ranging from one to six or more.

We then polled to see how many words they actually had in common. With very few exceptions, the result was

> ❖ The beginning of wisdom is the definition of terms.   —*Plato*

zero. Most people are quite surprised by this, not only by the lack of a single common word, but by the wide variety of interpretations they encounter when they engage in this exercise. These results have been consistent in workshops over many years with tens of thousands of consultants.

Perhaps we should not be surprised. Thomas Davenport, in his book *Information Ecology*, states, "The more an organization knows about a term or concept relevant to the business, the less likely it is to agree on a common term or meaning for it."

> ❖ When we listen to someone talk, the brain is constantly making assumptions—hundreds of them. Each word, gesture, inflection, and tone of voice is interpreted, but not always as the speaker intended. We usually are not aware of the fact that we are selecting one meaning from a number of possibilities.   —*Paul Swets, The Art of Talking So People Will Listen*

Assumptions are another form of guessing. They are particularly insidious because they often happen unconsciously; we do not even realize we are guessing. For example, in the Key Beliefs chapter we looked at numerous potential assumptions involved in the simple phrase "The solution to the problem is . . ."

To avoid guessing and assuming, it is helpful to listen carefully to the *key* words or phrases clients use, and then ask what those words mean to them. It is astounding how often clients respond with something very different from what we expect, or at least with something very useful and illuminating.

Let's say we are selling "data warehousing" solutions and the client asks if we "do" data warehousing. Rather than immediately launch into our presentation, we might first want to apply the principle of no guessing:

> CLIENT: "We are interested in data warehousing. Do you do that?"
> CONSULTANT: "We do. And interestingly enough, when I talk to ten different CIOs, I get ten different descriptions of what data warehousing means in their unique situation. Do you mind if I ask: when you say data warehousing, what does that mean to you in the context of what you are trying to achieve?"

The client gets a chance to explain what the company is trying to achieve, and we have the opportunity to learn more. Instead of mutual mystification, we get mutual understanding.

No Guessing: Challenge One

Write down several words or phrases commonly used in your line of business and for which there are multiple meanings and interpretations. The next ten times you hear someone say one of those words, ask the person what he or she means. Keep note of how often people come up with something either very surprising or very useful.

Consultants often do not ask these types of questions because they fear that they might seem ignorant—or seem as though *they* do not understand the term. In the foregoing example, you are not saying you do not know what data warehousing means in general; you are merely taking the time to understand what it means to the *client*. Instead of being perceived as ignorant, the consultant is often seen as concerned, caring, and someone who pays attention.

No Guessing: Challenge Two

After your next meeting with a client (by phone or face-to-face), take a few minutes to write down all of the assumptions that went unchallenged. How many might be critical? Repeat the procedure for at least five interactions.

The Questions We Never Ask

Often a question forms in our mind and, for whatever reason, we do not ask it. We then guess about the answer. Sometimes the questions are minor curiosities; often they are mission critical. They may be "the moose on the table" questions—questions that are essential to doing business or not, to succeeding or not—yet seem potentially embarrassing or challenging to ask.

> ❖ "It is about making the undiscussable discussable, about not taking for granted what is taken for granted, about getting the underground aboveground so that the unmanageable can become manageable." —Chris Argyris, Overcoming Organizational Defenses

With awareness and choice we can improve our ability to ask hard questions in a soft way:

> ❖ I am prejudiced in favor of him who, with impudence can ask boldly. He has faith in humanity and faith in himself.   —Johan Kaspar Lavater

Awareness: What are the questions I want to ask, yet do not?
Choice: How can I ask those questions in a way that both I and the client could feel good about?

No Guessing: Challenge Three

In your next several conversations, whether personal or professional, make a conscious effort to ask the questions you find yourself hesitating to ask. Notice which questions you still refuse to ask. Is there a pattern? What is stopping you? What would have to happen before you would ask the question? Can you find a low-risk opportunity to try?

SLOW DOWN FOR YELLOW LIGHTS

When you are driving, particularly when you are anxious to arrive somewhere important, and you encounter a yellow light, what do you do? If you are like many people, you go faster. Yellow lights have almost become the universal symbol for "Speed up!" Unfortunately, we use that same response with our clients. We hear something that concerns us, see a reaction that spells potential trouble, feel we are running into difficulty, then speed up to avoid running into our own worst fears.

The authors conducted a win/loss analysis for a client concerning a billion dollar outsourcing opportunity. The outsourcing firm and the prospective client each spent several million dollars to get to the point of a final proposal. The process took eighteen months. In the very first meetings a key group from the prospective client brought up a yellow light: "We think we can achieve the same cost reductions ourselves, without outsourcing." That yellow light was not dealt with then, nor dealt with during the subsequent eighteen months, and, unfortunately, was not dealt with effectively during the final presentation. The deal died a violent death. Postmortem interviews revealed that this was indeed a difficult yellow light to turn green and yet there were strong, viable resolutions that were never uncovered or pursued.

If hitting a red light on the road of opportunity is unavoidable, when would we like to hit it? As soon as possible! Intellectually, we know this; emotionally, we resist it. Perhaps we feel that hitting a red light is failure, and nobody likes to fail. Red lights are not failure! Failure is making red lights needlessly more expensive. A red light emerging late in the game usually means one or more yellow lights were ignored early on.

During conversations with clients, they will give us signals about how they are feeling and what they are thinking. Those signals will come verbally (what they say to you), vocally (how they say it—their inflection, emphasis, tone, pace), and visually (their nonverbal communication). As professional communicators, we need the *awareness* to sense these signals and the ability to intelligently *choose* how to deal with them.

Damn the Yellow Lights, Full Speed Ahead

Following is an example, from Mahan's professional experience, of what not to do in a yellow light situation. It is followed by a more exemplary case history.

One day I was calling on a large financial services firm. I had invited an important partner from a large consulting firm to accompany me—so I could show off my tremendous talents. (That was the first yellow light—I definitely did *not* check my ego at the door.) We were supposed to meet with the person championing our cause, as well as the chief executive officer and a vice president of marketing. When we arrived, we were informed that my champion, who was to fly in for the meeting, was not going to be there. (That was the second yellow light, but I moved right ahead.) As we were escorted up to the offices, we were informed that the CEO also could not make the meeting. (Major yellow light.) If I had not invited the consulting VIP to accompany me, I would have called off the meeting. It turns out that I should have called it off, and did not.

We then proceeded to meet with the vice president of marketing. At this point I was angry, upset, and knew I was talking to the wrong person. I plowed ahead anyway. I did my best to focus on the issues at hand. The vice president was very polite and answered all of my questions, yet every neuron in my brain and body was screaming, "This is going nowhere!" It was a scene resplendent with yellow lights, multiple and flashing.

If I had had my wits about me instead of my ego, I would have said, "John, you are being very polite and courteous, yet my intuition is telling me that this is going nowhere, and that after I walk out the door, nothing of substance will occur. What are you feeling at this point?" On this particular occasion, I lacked both clarity and courage. I said nothing, and sure enough, nothing happened. I was not fearless or flexible, and I did not have fun.

I later found out that the vice president had selected another firm in advance, had committed to them, and did everything in his power to make sure I did not talk to the CEO or anyone else. As it turned out, the competitor's solution did not meet the company's needs. It failed miserably. The vice president was let go, but this was no solace to me, given my inability to practice what I teach (and what I usually do).

Even if I had slowed down for the yellow lights, there was no guarantee that I could have turned them to green, but at least I could have tried. I would have had a chance to deal with what was really going on. The move to green or red would have been conscious and participatory rather than passive.

On the flip side, I once observed a visit by the head of a regional consulting firm to the newly appointed CEO of a highly desirable potential client. This CEO had recently worked for one of the major international consulting firms, which happened to have offices in the same building. The obvious yellow light was that this large project could go to the CEO's former firm, and my client would have the wonderful experience of spending lots of money on a proposal that had no chance. He had the courage to say what he was feeling. The conversation went something like this:

CONSULTANT: Frank, if I were in your shoes, I imagine that I might give preference on this type of a project to people I know and trust, such as my old firm. Have you at all been headed in that direction?

POTENTIAL CLIENT: That's certainly a consideration.

CONSULTANT: Well, let's deal with that head-on. What would you have to see, hear, or experience from us that would be so compelling that this would be at least a tough choice?

With some time and skill, the consultant was able to elicit the details that would make a difference, demonstrate them, and win the account.

The rule with yellow lights is: *If you see it, hear it, or feel it, find a way to say it—tactfully.*

State the Obvious

Yellow lights are doubts, stalls, concerns, fears, objections, or tough questions. They can be raised by either the client or you. Yellow lights can be obvious: "We don't have any budget for this"; "The CEO will never buy in"; "We've been working with your competitor for ten years, and we love them, but we want to see your proposal." Yellow lights can be subtle: we sense a lack of congruence between the words they say and how they say them; their nonverbal language is disquieting; something in your gut signals trouble. Yellow lights are often indicators that even if you have a solution that exactly meets the client's needs, the client will not buy it. Or you may feel you will not be able to construct a solution that exactly meets the client's needs because of a client belief, action, or lack of action. Pay attention and slow down.

> ❖ If you feel it, hear it, see it, find a way to say it—tactfully.

One powerful choice is to state the obvious, without undue emotional charge. Here is a three-part response that works well:

1. "I have a concern." (Or, "I am confused." Or, "I think we may have a problem.")
2. State the concern, the confusion, or the potential problem. State the fatal flaw that *prevents* arriving at a solution that exactly meets their needs, or express your sense that *even if* you get a viable solution, *even if* you produce the desired outcomes, it will not be adopted.
3. Ask what they think should happen next.

Here are some quick examples of how to use this three-part response to slow down for yellow lights. (We will explore yellow lights in more depth as we move through the ORDER process.)

Yellow light: The client requests a feature you don't provide:

1. "I think we may have a problem."
2. "We do everything else you've mentioned, and do it well. We don't do X, and don't plan to in the near future."
3. "What do you think we should do?"
   Green light (from client): "We should keep talking; that feature is not very important."
   Red Light (from client): "If you don't have that feature, it's a deal breaker."

Yellow light: You feel the client may have already decided:

1. "I'm getting a feeling I'd like to check out with you."
2. "Our only goal is to get you a solution that exactly meets your needs.

I'm sensing you feel you already have one, and the decision has already been made."

3. "Do you really need a proposal from us?"

Green light: They convince you there is something that would make a difference, that there are things you could do that would make the decision a tough choice.

Red light: They tell you, directly or indirectly, that the decision has been made or that there is nothing that would make a difference.

Yellow light: The client seems uncertain about whether they can get buy-in from key stakeholders:

1. "I have a concern."
2. "It sounds like even if we have a solution that exactly meets your needs, even if we can produce the results we've talked about, it won't be adopted unless these key stakeholders buy in."
3. "What do you feel we should do?"

A more subtle example of a yellow light might be something like the client continually glancing at his or her watch. You could say: "I noticed you glanced at your watch. Do we have a time constraint?" Or "I get the feeling that what I've suggested doesn't really interest you. Are we still on track or have we drifted?"

Green light: They are looking at their watch for an unrelated reason.
Red light: You lost them long ago and they cannot wait for this to end.

Red Lights

Red lights are not bad—they are just red lights. They do not even mean the opportunity is over. They do mean that we have hit a deal stopper which, if unresolved, will mean it is over. At least we are aware of what is going on and can

> ❖ Red lights are not failure. Failure is making red lights needlessly more expensive.

exercise some choices. Remember that a red light is not failure. Failure is when we make red lights needlessly more expensive.

Seek First to Understand

To qualify is to develop mutual understanding. Understanding dramatically increases in proportion to our ability to question and to listen.

Effective Questioning

Good questions unite the intelligence, emotional, and execution quotients:

IQ : Good questions do not merely elicit information the client already knows; they provoke a deeper exploration and insight on the part of the client. Good questions demonstrate our knowledge, expertise, and credibility more effectively than claims and statements.

EQ: Questions are "good" in large part because of how they are asked. Good questioners consistently create an atmosphere of trust; they have the ability to ask hard questions in a soft way. Their questions may be intellectually and emotionally challenging, yet they are worded and delivered in a manner that helps the client feel safe in responding.

XQ: Good questions are not random; they are organized in a logical progression in which questions and answers build on each other. Mutual understanding is like a jigsaw puzzle. Good questions elicit individual pieces of the puzzle. Good questioners have an effective methodology for fitting the pieces together. They fit more pieces in less time. They often complete the puzzle when others do not. Last but not least, putting the puzzle together with them is lot more enjoyable.

Effective Listening

The subsequent chapters on qualifying concentrate on the IQ, EQ, and XQ of good questions. What they do not cover, and what is usually the biggest constraint in arriving at mutual understanding, is our inability to accurately listen. If you cannot ask good questions, you may have little to listen to; if you cannot listen, you can't ask good questions and you won't deeply understand.

Good listening is a challenge and good listeners are rare. How many of us have been trained in good listening skills? How many have developed our listening "muscle" to an Olympic level? How many can *demonstrate,* rather than claim, good listening? How many of us even know what good listening is?

This following story by Charlotte Joko Beck, a respected author and teacher of Zen meditation, sheds light on the nature of the listening challenge.

Many years ago I was a piano major at Oberlin Conservatory. I was a very good student; not outstanding, but very good. And I very much wanted to study with one teacher who was undoubtedly the best. He'd take ordinary students and turn them into fabulous pianists. Finally I got my chance to study with *the* teacher.

When I went in for my lesson, I found that he taught with two pianos. He didn't even say hello. He just sat down at his piano and played five notes, and then he said, "You do it." I was supposed to play it just the way he played it. I played it—and he said, "No." He played it again, and I played it again. Again he said, "No." Well, we had an hour of that. And each time he said, "No."

In the next three months I played about three measures, perhaps half a minute of music. Now I had thought I was pretty good: I'd played soloist with the little symphony orchestras. Yet we did this for three months, and I cried most of those three months. He had all the marks of a real teacher, that tremendous drive and determination to make the student see. That's why he was so good. And at the end of the three months, one day he said, "Good." What had happened? Finally, I had learned to listen. And as he said, if you can hear it, you can play it.

What had happened in those three months? I had the same set of ears I started with; nothing had happened to my ears. What I was playing was not technically difficult. What had happened was that I had learned to listen for the first time . . . and I'd been playing the piano for many years. I learned to pay attention. That was why he was such a great teacher: he taught his students to pay attention. After working with him they really heard, they really listened. When you can hear it, you can play it. And, finished, beautiful pianists would finally come out of his studio.

When You Hear It, You Can Play It

Consultants frequently don't hear *exactly* what clients are saying and how they are saying it. This is the authors' conclusion after interacting with thousands of highly skilled consultants both in the field and in workshops. Consultants are not able to feed back key words and phrases that the client uses repeatedly; they do not explore the significance of those words more deeply. They use their own words rather than the client's and thus don't speak the client's language. They cannot repeat the client's metaphors and analogies; they then do not use those same metaphors to advocate their own ideas and beliefs, thus missing out on a powerful means of communication. They do not emulate the client's speed of talking, intonation, inflection, or emphasis; they lose the opportunity to create a deep level of rapport by speaking in a comparable fashion. They do not hear when there is a lack of alignment between what clients say, how they say it, and what they look like when they say it. Consultants lose the ability to understand the source of that incongruence, which can be critical to understanding. They do not hear "what is not being said," the "meaning between the words," the unspoken communication; they deal only with the tip of the communication

> ❖ Are you hearing *exactly* what the client is saying—and not saying?

iceberg that appears above the surface and not with the richness of complexity below; their understanding is shallow rather than deep.

We are always listening. However, we are often listening to the voice inside our own head. We ask a good question, and instead of listening to the answer, we start thinking of the next question. The client is talking, but we are listening to the running commentary in our mind. We may even have multiple voices going on inside. Those voices might be brilliant, they might be highly engaging and entertaining—they just don't happen to be the client's voice.

> ❖ Listening requires awareness: whose voice are you listening to— yours or the client's?
>
> ❖ Listening requires sustained concentration—you must pay attention with all of your senses.

Listening requires choice and concentration. Expert listeners consciously choose which voice they pay attention to—their internal voice or the client's. If we stay present and alert, and turn down the volume of the internal voice, we can concentrate all of our senses on the external communication—the exact words and how they are said. Then we truly listen. If we combine keen listening with good questions, we can foster a rich level of mutual understanding.

**Listening requires choice
and concentration**

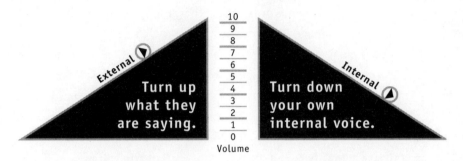

Stay aware. Whose voice are you hearing?

Many of us, like Ms. Beck prior to meeting her teacher, are very good at what we do. We have two good ears and feel we are quite competent at listening. This is part of the challenge: how do we get better at something we do not know we are bad at? A book cannot teach you to be a good listener. Go out and find teachers. Practice with your significant other, a friend, or a colleague. Make it a goal to hear *exactly* what people are saying. You might be amazed by the results. You might learn a lot more about people than you ever thought was possible. You might genuinely enjoy the increased ability to stay present, to remain alert and focused; you might find that those abilities apply meaningfully to many areas of your life.

CHAPTER THREE

QUALIFYING OPPORTUNITIES

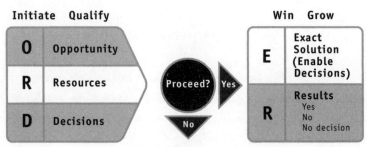

The penalty for poor qualification is severe. One research firm estimates that 65 percent of salespeople are pursuing worthless deals. How productive is that? Eighty percent of lost sales opportunities are a result of an inadequate or nonexistent qualification process and the lack of an effective sales planning process. Yet frequently the response to that failure is to increase the number of opportunities pursued rather than the quality of the qualification process. When we chase low-probability opportunities, our win rate goes down and our costs go up.

The dialogue around Opportunity is of particular importance. Most situations require that we have the Opportunity conversation with the many individuals who will influence the decisions and allocate the resources. Each person will have a perspective on a solution that will exactly meet their company's needs. If there is not a strongly perceived Opportunity, nothing else matters.

THE OPPORTUNITY CHECKLIST

The authors offer the following Opportunity Checklist to aid in the mutual understanding of the Opportunity.

> **Issues:** What problems or results is the client trying to address? In what priority?
> **Evidence:** How do we define the problem? How do we measure success?
> **Impact:** What are the financial and intangible costs and benefits?
> **Context:** Who or what else is affected by the issues and the solution?
> **Constraints:** What has stopped (or might stop) the organization from resolving these issues?

The Opportunity Checklist points to what we want to know in order to qualify the opportunity; structuring the conversation is a questioning process to efficiently elicit that information.

STRUCTURING THE OPPORTUNITY CONVERSATION

To structure the conversation:

> Move off the solution.
> Get out *all* of the issues.
> Prioritize the issues.
> Gather evidence and impact.
> Explore context and constraints.

The rest of this chapter examines in depth each element of a structured opportunity conversation and gives examples of how to ask effective questions. The discussion proceeds in a linear and logical manner. While there is good reason for this sequence of events, there is no need to follow this particular order in a conversation. The aim is to cover the Opportunity Checklist in a way that is natural and conversational, that resonates well with the client, and that is time efficient. A good rule and practice is to "Start anywhere, go everywhere." Let the tool serve you; do not serve the tool.

Move off the Solution

STRUCTURE THE CONVERSATION

Move off the solution
Get out all of the issues
Prioritize the issues
Gather evidence and impact
Explore content and constraints

If you have not read Key Belief No. 3 (Solutions have no inherent value), please do so now. If you have read it, give it a quick review.

Some neuroscientists and psychologists tell us that human beings are wired to pay attention and exert effort in response to one of three key stimuli: pain, gain, novelty. We want less pain and will move away from it. We want more gain and will move toward it. We notice what is new in our environment and will pay attention to it until we assess whether it moves us away from pain or toward gain. Despite the opinion of certain consultants, clients *are* human beings. They are unlikely to move toward any of our solutions if they are not experiencing an unacceptable amount of pain or strongly seeking meaningful new gain. The short and sweet rule of qualifying the Opportunity is: No pain, no gain = no opportunity.

> ❖ No pain, no gain = no opportunity.

In a business context, the word "problem" is a synonym for pain; the word "result" is a synonym for gain. The authors use the word "issue" for *either* a problem or a result; consequently, as used here, an issue can be either negative or positive.

The *intent* of moving off the solution is to better understand the issues that the solution must address. If you cannot find important problems or desired results, you probably have low client motivation and a low-probability Opportunity. The following section describes how to move off a solution requested by the client.

The formula for moving off the solution is: listen, soften, move:

The formula for *Move off the Solution* is:

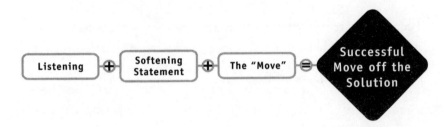

Listen: We want to hear *exactly* how the client describes the requested solution.

Soften: When people ask us a question, they expect our response to fit into the recognized pattern of an answer. Answering a question with a question breaks this expected pattern and it may seem harsh, abrupt, or elusive. It is more effective if we begin our response with a softening statement, and then ask our question.

Move: Ask a question that invites the client to describe the underlying problems or desired results that the solution is intended to address.

Examples of "Soften"

The client asks you to tell them about your solution:

"I'd be glad to. In order to keep my comments relevant to your situation, could I ask ...?"

"Sure. I could talk for several hours with great enthusiasm—and that may not be what you want. Do you mind if I ask ...?"

"We've helped many companies address business problems with (the requested solution) and each one had different priorities and objectives. Would it be okay if we started out talking a bit about ...?"

Examples of "Move"

> "What kinds of problems have you been experiencing by not having . . . ?"

> "Let's say you put in a world-class solution and it was working well. What would that allow you to do as a business that you can't do today?"

People who are trying to "move away from pain" will probably give you a list of problems (challenges, frustrations, concerns, dissatisfactions). They may even use physical or emotional pain phrases like: "It's killing us . . . ," "We're bleeding . . . ," "It's a pain in the neck . . . ," "It's a real headache . . . ," "It's a nightmare . . . ," "It's like pulling teeth. . . ." People who are "moving toward gain" will respond with results (goals, outcomes, objectives, benefits). They may use phrases like: "What we'd like to see . . . ," "What we think is possible . . . ," "Our vision is . . . ," "What we're excited about is . . . ," "We'd like to create . . . ," etc. Their language gives you some hints about whether they are more motivated by pain or gain.

Here are two examples of moving off the solution:

EXAMPLE 1

Client: "We need a company-wide ERP system and are unsure whether to go with an off-the-shelf implementation or develop a customized solution. We feel we have a lot of unique needs. What would you recommend?

> ❖ MOVE OFF THE SOLUTION!

OPTION 1: NO GUESSING

"I'd be glad to share our experience. Before we get too far down the path, ERP is a term that has come to mean different things to different people—anything from systems that cover an entire organization to just a set of specific modules. When you say you want a company-wide ERP system, what specifically does that mean to you in the context of what you are trying to achieve?"

> ❖ No guessing: what meaning do they attach to their key words and phrases?

OPTION 2: MOVE TO THE PROBLEMS

"I'd be glad to share our experience. We've had the opportunity to help many companies in your industry select and implement ERP systems. I heard you say you have unique needs. In order to keep my comments relevant to your situation, could you help me understand what specific kinds of challenges you've been experiencing that you are hoping an ERP system will resolve?"

> ❖ Problems: what bad things happen if there is no solution?

OPTION 3: MOVE TO THE RESULTS

"I'd be glad to share our experience. We've had the opportunity to help many companies in your industry select and implement ERP systems. I heard you say you have unique needs. Let's say we are a year down the road, the ERP system is implemented and working well. What will you be able to do at that time as a business that you can't do today?

> ❖ Results: what good things will they get with the solution that they can't get today?

EXAMPLE 2

Client: "We need to optimize our supply chain for the greatest efficiencies, so we can better serve our customers. What are some common recommendations you offer in this type of situation?"

OPTION 1: NO GUESSING

"I'd be glad to share our experience. Most of our recommendations are customized, partly because supply chain has so many diverse elements that it means different things to different organizations. You said you need to 'optimize the supply chain to better serve your customers.' Can you give me a little background on what that's come to mean in your organization?"

OPTION 2: MOVE TO THE PROBLEMS

"I'd be glad to share our experience. While there are common principles of good supply chain management, for them to be effective they need to be adapted to the specific needs of an organization. I want to keep my comments relevant to your situation. Will you share with me some areas where you feel you are not as optimized or efficient as you could be?"

OPTION 3: MOVE TO THE RESULTS

"I'd be glad to share our experience. There are common principles of good supply chain management, and for them to be effective they need to be tailored to the specific needs of an organization. If I heard correctly, a desired outcome for you is to better serve your customers. Let's say you were to optimize and gain greater supply chain efficiencies. How would you expect that to generate better results with your customers?"

In each example, we talk about the problems to be solved and/or the results to be achieved rather than about the solution. No pain, no gain . . . no meaningful opportunity.

EXERCISE

Step 1: Write down three to five ways your clients typically request a solution.
Step 2: For each of these ways, write out a "Move off the Solution" response. Vary your responses a bit.
Step 3: Practice your responses until they are completely natural.

Get Out All of the Issues

STRUCTURE THE CONVERSATION

Move off the solution
Get out all of the issues
Prioritize the issues
Gather evidence and impact
Explore content and constraints

When we invite the client to move off the solution, they either move or don't move. If they *do* move, there are usually multiple issues rather than just one. Consultants have a strong tendency to start talking in depth about the first issue mentioned. It is often helpful to exert the patience and discipline to get out *all* of the issues first, as long as the client is willing. We can then talk about them in order of importance to the client.

If you immediately explore the first issue mentioned instead of getting a complete list, you risk the following:

1. You will never get the complete list, and thus may miss significant opportunities.
2. You will end up talking about an issue that is not the most important issue.
3. Even if you do eventually discover the most important issue, you may have wasted the scarce resources of time and energy.

Give the client verbal and nonverbal recognition, confirmation, and appreciation when they give you an item for the list. Let them know that it is helpful. Nod your head up and down. Show them lightbulbs of dawning comprehension in your expressions. In other words, don't just robotically collect the list.

It is helpful to periodically summarize what the client is saying and to use his or her words rather than your own. You can feed back what you have heard to make sure you got it right, and that you didn't leave anything out. When the client finishes the list, *you* might have some additional issues that you think are candidates for the list; you can offer these in a non-leading way: "Other clients facing issues like these have also been wrestling with [give examples]. Has that at all been an issue for you?"

When you sense the list is finished, you can test for completeness by asking, "Let's say you were able to address all these issues successfully—and nothing else. Would that be a solution that exactly met your needs?" When clients think for a bit, they sometimes come up with additional items that can be surprisingly important.

Prioritize the Issues

STRUCTURE THE CONVERSATION

Move off the solution
Get out all of the issues
Prioritize the issues
Gather evidence and impact
Explore content and constraints

❖ Find out which issue is most important to the client.

Once we have completed the list, we can prioritize the issues. We can say, "I'm sure all of these issues are important and interrelated. Is there one that you feel has the most leverage or impact?" When the client picks one, you can then go into depth on evidence and impact.

Rule of thumb: Eighty percent of the impact is in 20 percent of the issues. You have limited conversational time with the client. When you prioritize, you can spend that time on the issues that are most important to the client.

❖ 80 percent of the impact is in 20 percent of the issues.

The client may have trouble selecting only one issue and say that they are all important. You can respond, "They *are* all important. I'll make sure we discuss them all. Which one would you like to talk about first?"

You do not have to prioritize all of the issues. Getting the top one or two priorities is enough to begin the discussion in more depth.

Gather Evidence and Impact

> **STRUCTURE THE CONVERSATION**
>
> Move off the solution
> Get out all of the issues
> Prioritize the issues
> **Gather evidence and impact**
> Explore content and constraints

For some reason, consultants often overlook evidence. Perhaps they hear the client's issue, know they can do something about it, and want to talk about the solution rather than more closely define the problem. Gathering evidence and impact is pivotal to building a good business case for the opportunity. A good business case bolsters the probability of success; a missing or inadequate business case is a yellow light.

Evidence defines problems and measures success. For a problem: How do we know it is a problem? What is there too much or too little of? By how much? Do they have *too little* profit, *too limited* revenue, *too many* complaints, *too many* rejects? For a result: How will we measure success? What must increase or decrease? By how much? If we do not understand which

> ❖ How do we know this to be true? Where is the evidence?

numbers are too small or too big, it will be difficult to understand which numbers our solution is supposed to increase or decrease.

How we ask evidence questions is guided by how the client phrases the issue. Some issues lend themselves immediately to measurement since they are subject to "hard numbers." The authors call them "hard" issues. Examples would be sales, costs, inventory turns, and productivity ratios. Other issues are difficult to measure or are subjective opinion. We call these "soft" issues. Examples would be employee morale, market awareness, strategic importance. Soft issues are not necessarily less important or less impactful; they are just harder to monetize.

"Hard" Issues

Many consultants do not translate client issues into monetary terms. Yet most issues *are* issues because they have financial repercussions. Problems cost money. Results provide money. How *much* money is the question. Nobody benefits when you leave the hard and real consequences of your clients' issues a mystery.

Your solution will have a price attached to it; that will not be a mystery. Both you and your clients will make better decisions when client issues are

> ❖ Show me the money!

monetized as well. The sooner you can talk about abstract notions in the concrete terms of money, the sooner you can address the issues in a tangible way.

Every company has measurables. They all have some form of financial measures, operational measures, performance measures, technology or process measures, customer satisfaction measures, etc. It is frustrating to listen to a consultant interview a client, have the client sprinkle the conversation with measurables, and watch the consultant not follow up on even one. We need to have finely tuned measurable alerts. When we hear something we can measure that is directly related to the issues the solution is supposed to resolve, our measurable alert should fire off and we should ask questions that put a dollar figure on the issue.

When you can readily translate a client priority into dollars, do so.

Hard issues can readily be converted to money. When an issue is "hard," ask the "Five Golden Questions":

1. How do you measure it?
2. What is it now?
3. What would you like it to be?
4. What is the value of the difference?
5. What is the value over time (over a reasonable management horizon—e.g., two to three years)?

Question five (What is the value over time?) is typically a confirming question from the consultant; you are not asking the client to do what is usually simple arithmetic. For example, if the annual "value of the difference" of excess inventory was $200,000, you might say, "So over a two- to three-year period you would be looking at $400,000–600,000 in excess inventory?" The objective is to state the value of the difference over a reasonable management horizon rather than by an arbitrary time period such as a year or month or quarter.

It sometimes makes sense to omit question one (How do you measure it?) and start with question two (What is it now?). In the examples that follow, start issues listed in the first column with "How do you measure _____?" For the second column, you might start with "What are _____ now?"

How do you measure _____?	What are _____ now?
Productivity	Sales
Quality	Costs
Customer Satisfaction	Margins
Employee Satisfaction	Profits
Effectiveness	Inventory turns
Efficiency	Time to market
Performance	Cycle time

You may want to insert the requested solution between questions two (What is it now?) and three (What would you like it to be?). For example, if the client is looking for software that allows it to increase widgets per hour, and it currently produces one thousand widgets per hour, you might ask, "If the software was in place and working the way you hoped, what number of widgets would you expect per hour?"

THE FIVE GOLDEN QUESTIONS

1. How do you measure it?
2. What is it now?
3. What would you like it to be?
4. What is the value of the difference?
5. What is the value over time?

Here's a simple example of the Five Golden Questions at work. The client says his biggest issue is deteriorating margins:

> CONSULTANT: That's a common challenge in the industry. What are your current margins?
> CLIENT: We are running at about 28 percent.
> CONSULTANT: And let's say you have the technology we discussed in place, and it is working they way you expect. What do you see as the impact on margins?
> CLIENT: We expect this initiative alone to get us up to a sustainable 30 percent.
> CONSULTANT: And that is a 2 percent gain on what level of sales?
> CLIENT: For the market we are targeting, we're looking at about $100 million a year.
> CONSULTANT: Thank you. That helps me gauge what you are trying to achieve. So $2 million a year over a two to three year period is about a $4–6 million improvement without allowing for increases in sales?
> CLIENT: Yes. And with sales growth that number will hopefully go up.

BACK OF THE ENVELOPE MATH

Sometimes it is easy to calculate the value of the difference. If current purchasing costs are $24 million and the client wants to reduce them to $20 million, even the authors can do the math. More difficult is measuring the monetary value of issues such as increased inventory turns, decreased employee turnover, and improved time to market. You are encouraged to increase your competence at "back of the envelope math" and to go for rough approximation rather than detailed accuracy. Use words and phrases like "ballpark," "rough estimate," "more or less," "best guess," "gut instinct." You want to at least know the order of magnitude: Is the client talking about tens of thousands of dollars, hundreds of thousands, millions, tens of millions, hundreds of millions? Turn all nondollar figures into dollars. Do not end up with percentages or ratios without explicitly converting them to money.

Here's another example of the Five Golden Questions. The client believes the key issue is "quality":

CONSULTANT: How do you measure quality?

CLIENT: We have a few measures, but the one we're looking at is number of rejections per thousand units.

CONSULTANT: Thanks. Out of curiosity, what is the current rejection rate?

CLIENT: Well, there are a lot of variations depending on circumstances. On the average, it's about ten per thousand units.

CONSULTANT: Let's say we were successful with this project. What would you expect it to be?

CLIENT: Our target is five per thousand units.

CONSULTANT: What does an extra five units per thousand mean in terms of dollars?

A this point, we may have a problem. We have just asked the client to do a lot of math in his or her head. It is helpful to do some "back of the envelope" math with the client to arrive at the amount. Here are two approaches:

CHUNKING IT DOWN

CONSULTANT: Roughly, what does it cost for one rejection?

CLIENT: Well, the cost accountants are always debating what the real cost is. Call it about a thousand dollars per rejection.

CONSULTANT: So that's five fewer rejections per thousand units times $1,000 per unit. You would save $5,000 per thousand units produced. How many units do you produce annually?

CLIENT: Three million, total.

CONSULTANT: Help me with the math. Three million divided by one thousand is three thousand. Three thousand times $5,000 is $15 million. Does that sound right?

CLIENT: Yeah, that's very close.

CONSULTANT: So over two to three years you are looking at somewhere between $30 million to $45 million wrapped up in this quality issue?

In chunking it down, we have allowed the client to go through the process *with* us so he or she understands the impact of the numbers as well as we do, and feels that the numbers are legitimate.

ROLLING IT UP

CONSULTANT: What do you spend on rejections each year—roughly, ballpark?

CLIENT: Tens of millions.

CONSULTANT: Closer to two or three, or closer to eight or nine?

CLIENT: About $25 to $30 million.

CONSULTANT: So, if you cut that in half you would save around $12.5 to $15 million a year?

CLIENT: That sounds right.

CONSULTANT: So over two to three years, you are looking at somewhere between $25 million to $45 million wrapped up in this quality issue?

Have the client run the numbers with you, or for you. Do not sit there with your financial calculator and spend five minutes punching buttons then announce, "Wow, you have a $20 million problem!" At that point, *they* do not have a $20 million problem, even if your numbers are right. *You and your financial calculator* have a $20 million problem. Gain client buy-in to the numbers by including them in the calculations.

> ❖ Have the client do the math with you or for you—or verbalize the math you do and make it easy to understand.

If the numbers come up big, do not gloat or give off the vibration of "Gotcha!" Be the conservative one. Say something like "That seems like a large number. Is that realistic?" That gives them a chance to either modify it and come up with a number they believe in, or to say something like, "Well, if anything, it's probably underestimated." Remember that the goal is not to "get them"—the goal is to get real.

Finding Evidence for Soft Issues

Soft issues, as we have defined them, do not immediately lend themselves to data driven evidence. We usually need to ask questions that help us determine how clients concluded they have a problem or would know that they had achieved important results. Two good words to help us gather such evidence are *how* and *what*. Following are some examples of how and what questions to elicit evidence for soft issues.

HOW—PROBLEM EVIDENCE

How does _____ show up as a problem?

How did you (or the company) become convinced that _____ is a problem?

If we did "management by walking around," how would someone demonstrate that _____ is a a problem?

If you had to make a business case to the CFO, how would you prove a problem exists?

And when you can't _____, how does that negatively impact your business?

WHAT—PROBLEM EVIDENCE

What lets you know _____ is a problem?

What measures, if any, prove that _____ is a problem?

What key performance indicators go up and down when _____?

If we were doing management by walking around, what would convince us that _____ is a problem?

And when you can't _____, then what happens?

HOW—RESULTS EVIDENCE

How specifically would you measure success?

How would you and others know we were successful?

Let's say you achieve what you want. Have you already thought about how you would like to measure a return on your investment?

Let's say we end up doing this together, how should we prove to key stakeholders this is a good idea?

And if you could _____, how would that benefit the business?

WHAT—RESULTS EVIDENCE

What would let you know we we successful?

What would be some good measures of success?

What indicators will increase or decrease if we are successful?

What would be your punch list for success?

And if you could _____, what would that allow you to do as a business that you can't do today?

And if you could ____, what would be the benefits?

Questions such as these can get us started toward understanding the nature of the problem and the definition of success.

Turning Soft Issues into Hard Currency

Soft issues are not necessarily less important. Nor are they "bad" because they are soft. They are merely difficult to measure or quantify. As such, it is hard to compare the hard dollars of the solution investment to the opinions and beliefs about the issue. It is harder for the client to make an intelligent buying decision.

Clients may say they want to improve communication, enhance competitive position, or have better relations with customers. Maybe they say they have a problem with morale, trust, or motivation. Perhaps they do not feel they are getting the most out of their people, their marketing, or their reputation in the marketplace. They might need a strategic approach, a better plan, creative thinking, more innovation, improved teamwork, or visionary leadership. How will we and the client quantify the value of these "soft" issues? It is often helpful to "peel the onion" in order to discover the "So what?" and "Who cares?" that lurk beneath the surface.

Our goal in peeling the onion is to move from a broad, generic description of an issue to the underlying motivation, or key driver. From an IQ perspective, we move from soft evidence to hard measures. From an EQ perspective, we move from that which is known, intellectual, and safe, to that which is unexamined, emotional, and possibly vulnerable. We are trying to get real about what makes this issue important—intellectually and emotionally.

> ❖ Peel for pain: When a bad thing happens, then what happens? What are the consequences? Who cares? For what reasons?

If you start with a problem—something the client wants to remove, avoid, or move away from—"peel for pain." You can say something like "And when this problem occurs, then what happens?" Other phrases for "Then what happens?" are: "And what does that affect?" "And what are the consequences of that?" "And what does that, in turn, impact?" "And how does that affect the bottom line?" "Worst-case scenario, if you never change this, what will happen?"

For example:

> CLIENT: We can't get one holistic view of our customer.
>
> CONSULTANT: [Listens carefully. Sounds like a soft issue.] Help me understand. When you can't get one holistic view of the customer, what happens?
>
> CLIENT: We provide widely different service depending on which person gets the call and what information they happen to have available.
>
> CONSULTANT: [Listens carefully. Still sounds soft.] And I'm hearing that's not a good thing. What are the consequences of widely different service?
>
> CLIENT: Our customers get frustrated and our reps are ineffective.
>
> CONSULTANT: Is one of those more of a concern than the other?
>
> CLIENT: Probably the customer frustration.
>
> CONSULTANT: [Still hearing soft.] I could guess but I won't. If customers stay frustrated, where does that show up in your performance?
>
> CLIENT: The number we're most concerned about is dollars per initial sale.
>
> CONSULTANT: [Finally hears a hard measure; begins the Five Golden Questions.] And your dollars-per-initial-sale level currently is . . . ?"

If you start with a result—something the client wants to achieve, obtain, or move toward—"peel for gain." Ask a question like "And if you could have this result, what would that allow you to do?" You can vary how you ask that question: "What does that get you?" "Where do the benefits of that show up?" "How does that impact performance?" "How does that help the bottom line?" "Best-case scenario, what will be the ultimate gain?" Keep stripping away layers until you get to something that is a key business driver (ideally, a hard measure), a key emotional driver, or both.

> ❖ Peel for gain: If a good thing happens, what will that allow them to do that they can't do today? Who benefits? What's the big deal?

For example:

> CLIENT: What we really need here is improved communication.
>
> CONSULTANT: [Listens; hears "soft."] Just so I can better understand

what's going on, let's say you improved your communication; what would that allow you to do that you can't do today?

CLIENT: For one thing, sales and production would be on the same page.

CONSULTANT: [Still hearing soft; hearing there might be other examples as well.] Well, let's look at that for a minute. If sales and production were consistently on the same page, what would be the big deal?

CLIENT: We could get some reasonably accurate sales forecasts; the ones we get now are notoriously bad.

CONSULTANT: [Still hearing soft.] You're not alone in that. And you would expect the biggest benefits of accurate forecasts to be ... ?

CLIENT: We wouldn't constantly overproduce or underproduce. If we don't overproduce we'll save on inventory costs and need fewer markdowns. If we don't underproduce we'll have fewer stock-outs and will make more sales. We'll never be perfect, but we could get much closer.

CONSULTANT: [Hears some measurables (inventory costs, markdowns, sales); asks the Five Golden Questions; remembers to ask about other benefits of good communication.]

If You Feel It, Ask It

The authors often observe that consultants who are attempting to peel the onion will get close to the last level of questioning and then, just before they get to the real impact or a measurable, they bail out with a safe question like "How many employees do you have?" or "What's your current version of the software?" Afterward, when the consultants are asked during the debriefing if they could hear in their minds what the next question should have been, they usually say, "Yes, but clearly the other person would have felt uncomfortable if I had asked that question."

During win/loss analysis, when the *client* is asked, "If the consultant had asked this question, what would have been your reaction?" they often say, "Tough question ... a good question though. I would have liked to talk about that."

The reason consultants frequently give for not getting to the heart of the matter is that they feel the *client* would feel uncomfortable. The real reason seems to be that the *consultant* would feel uncomfortable. The irony is that we wait to establish rapport before asking the hard question, yet asking the hard question can help us establish rapport.

> ❖ Often we wait for rapport before asking the hard question when often asking the hard question (in a soft way) creates rapport.

It is not as if clients know their eventual response and are just waiting for you to discover it. Often they have not been through the intellectual or emotional inquiry to figure out the real consequence of their situation. Getting to the heart of the matter provides added value to the client, not just more information to you.

If You Can't Quantify, Qualify

It is almost always helpful to quantify the impact. Since the solution you will provide is priced in currency, it is helpful for the issues it addresses to be at least roughly described in currency as well. Quantifying helps clients make better decisions. It makes it easier to defend their opinions to others in the organization.

Sometimes, however, it is difficult or inappropriate to quantify the impact of an issue. Clients may not have the patience, discipline, trust, or willingness to quantify the impact. Our rule, then, is, *"If you cannot quantify, at least strongly qualify."* One way to qualify is to use a scale of one to ten. We put a numeric qualifier on a feeling or belief.

> ❖ If you can't quantify (and even if you can), qualify importance on a scale of 1–10.

This gives both us and the client more accuracy about the importance and/or urgency of that belief, and greater facility in comparing it to what others believe.

A sample form of the question is: "On a scale of one to ten—with ten being that it is mission-critical and you have to do it, and one being that it's irritating, but you can live with it—where are you?"

If they say they are an eight, nine, or ten, the issue is important and motivating. If they are six or less, it is a yellow light. A seven is enough to keep us talking and not enough to make it a "no brainer."

To summarize: If the issue is hard, ask the Five Golden Questions. If the issue is soft, peel the onion until you can ask the Five Golden Questions. If you cannot quantify, strongly qualify on a scale of one to ten.

A Predictable Path

When we ask the client for evidence, *either they have it or they do not.* It is surprising to find that even when we are talking to people intimately connected to the issues, they often can't come up with evidence, or the evidence is soft. When the client does not have evidence, *either someone else does or nobody does.* If someone else does, the logical questions are "Who?" and "When can we talk to them?" This is an opportunity to move from people who do not know to people who do.

If *nobody* has the evidence, an appropriate question is "Is evidence important?" Is it helpful and important to get this evidence in order to build a good business case for the solution? If it is important to get the evidence, *can they get it themselves or do they need some help?* Often they will say that they need some help. At this point, the client has sold themselves on a diagnostic. The rule of thumb is that when information is important and the client has not been able to get it on their own, 80 percent of the time they will want some help.

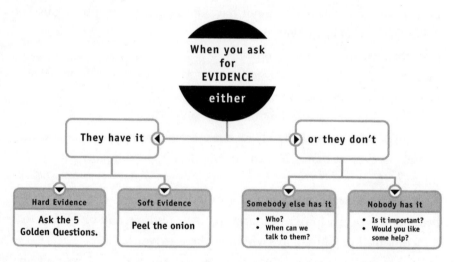

Sometimes evidence is not important to the people we are talking to. Perhaps they live with the situation every day and do not need data to know it's a problem. Yet, often these people have to go to others in the organization to get funding. Those other people do not live with the situation every day and are likely to allocate resources based on a good business case. The lack of a good business case can result in either no funds being allocated or an insufficient amount of funds being allocated to address the issue. So even if the person we talk to does not need the evidence, someone else might.

When the Impact Is . . .

It bears repeating: About 80 percent of the impact is in 20 percent of the issues. After covering the top one or two issues, we should be coming to some initial judgments:

The impact seems big (relative to the likely investment)
The impact seems small (relative to the likely investment)
There is disagreement on the impact

When the impact is big: Be curious about the constraints. Ask the client: "What has stopped the organization from realizing these benefits before now?" (See Explore Context and Constraints)

> ❖ When the impact is big, ask for the constraints. When the impact is small, take away the solution and see what happens.

When the impact is small: At any point in our discussions with the client, either one of us might reach the conclusion that the impact of the opportunity is not substantial. For whatever reason, if we sense the opportunity is either not important or not urgent, we can exercise two choices:

1. Say so.
2. Take away the solution.

It might sound something like any of the following:

"Tom, if this problem is only costing you $100,000 a year, the problem may be cheaper than the solution. Let's say you did nothing, and just watched this over the next couple of years—would anyone even care?"

"Linda, if this rates only a "five," doesn't it seem likely that the company would be better off spending its money on eights, nines, and tens?"

"You've been working with XYZ for five years. They are a good company. Why not stay with them?"

"It sounds like there is a huge downside if this fails. Is it possible to eliminate the risk by just not doing the project?"

"It sounds like this is something you could handle very well in-house. Would there be any reason not to do that?"

Likely Reactions

When you take away the solution, the client is apt to do one of two things: 1. Let it go.
  2. Fight for it.

If they decide to let it go, did you lose the business? You can't lose something you never had. You were likely to lose the business anyway; you just would have made your loss more expensive. If they are willing to let it go, you should be too.

If they fight for it, they have to convince *us* to propose the solution, rather than us convincing them. It is more powerful when people convince themselves. The old cliché is "If you say it, it's sold; if they say it, it's gold." People love to buy; they hate to be sold. It is amusing to see the consultant try to talk the client out of doing something while the client comes up with more and more reasons for moving ahead. Amusing or not, it is often useful to take away the solution.

Remember that intent counts more than technique. If your intent is to get a solution that exactly meets the client's needs, to be authentic, and to stay attuned to what is showing up rather than what you would like to hear, you will be able to take away the solution and be thoroughly congruent. "If you aren't ready to walk, you're not ready to talk."

WHEN THE IMPACT IS NOT AGREED UPON

Sometimes the client is willing to give up the solution, yet we think they are making a mistake. We see the impact as being greater than they do. At this point, we have little to lose; if they do not change their perception of the impact, we will not be able to help them. It is appropriate at this point to ask some more questions and/or give them the information that we think they lack. Either we will come to agree with them that the impact is small and offer gracefully to exit, or they will agree with us that the impact is big, and we can choose to continue. Or we will agree to disagree and will be at a yellow or red light.

For example, let's say that a client has evidence that employee turnover in a key segment of her company is significantly higher than industry standards; her company is at 38 percent versus only 20 percent for the industry. However, she doesn't attribute any adverse impact to the "high" turnover; the 38 percent statistic doesn't trouble her. Perhaps she is right and it is not a problem (and it is not a problem until the client says it is). Perhaps neither she nor others in her company have computed the direct and opportunity costs of that amount of turnover, and would be more concerned if they knew what they were up against.

We can ask questions and provide information about turnover such as in the accompanying chart. In doing so, we keep an open and objective mind. We are not trying to prove we are right and they are wrong. We are trying to mutually understand if the amount of turnover is really a problem or if we should cross it off the list of issues.

When the impact is not agreed upon, ask questions and/or provide information

Opportunity Costs?
If costs were down and productivity up, how would you use the resulting rewards?

Hiring Costs?
- Agencies
- Company time

Lost Productivity?
- Lower percentage of experienced workers
- Less flexibility in job switching

Reputation Down?
- "Can't keep people."
- Harder to hire with bad reputation for retaining people?

Higher Error Rate?

More Non-Value-Added Paperwork?
It costs to move people in and out of the company

High Turnover

More Accidents?

Training Costs?
- Time for new people
- Time of trainers
- Loss of production

Higher Unemployment Taxes?

Higher Cost of Temporary Help?

Less Customer Satisfaction?
"I'm always dealing with someone different."

Explore Context and Constraints

```
┌─────────────────────────────────────────┐
│                                          │
│   STRUCTURE THE CONVERSATION             │
│   ─────────────────────────              │
│                                          │
│   Move off the solution                  │
│   Get out all of the issues              │
│   Prioritize the issues                  │
│   Gather evidence and impact             │
│   Explore content and constraints        │
│                                          │
└─────────────────────────────────────────┘
```

Context

Calculating impact is important in helping buyers make good business decisions. As we explore context, we may broaden and deepen our evaluation of the impact.

There are two types of context that are helpful to explore: organizational and operational.

ORGANIZATIONAL

How does this initiative fit into the big picture? How does it connect with:

- Mission
- Values
- Key strategies and initiatives
- External and internal pressures
- Political landscape

> ❖ Organizational context: How does this initiative fit into the big picture?

What is going on in the company that affects every decision made, not just the one being discussed? Every company has an explicit or implicit mission; it has values; it has key initiatives or strategies it believes will make the company successful. What are they and how do they relate to our solution? Projects that align with organizational context make more sense to more people and are less price-sensitive. To the degree that our solutions help meet companywide goals, it will help many people and efforts, not just a few.

OPERATIONAL

When we intervene in one part of a system, it usually has ramifications and ripple effects in other parts of the organization. Solutions rarely exist in isolation. Consultants need to be aware of the interconnections in the client's ecosystem. If we are going to change one part of the system, we should know who or what else is affected by our solution.

> ❖ Operational context: Who or what else is affected?

The basic tenets of systems thinking have been thoroughly examined by numerous authors. The goal here is not to review them; it is to encourage ourselves to learn and apply them in our work with clients. The more we think systemically, the more likely it is we will have a solution that truly works for the whole and is sustainable over time.

The key question we are trying to answer here is "Who or what else is affected by this issue (these issues, the implementation of the solution)?" For instance, we might ask, "Does this affect just you and your department, or does it affect other departments as well?" or, "Does this affect just this process, or does it impact other processes as well?"

When we explore context, we may find additional opportunities to help the client. If we cannot help them ourselves, we can make the client aware of our strategic partners in whom we have confidence.

Exploring context might also reveal the existence of key influencers and decision makers whose input is important, and whose names might not otherwise appear.

Constraints

WHEN THE IMPACT SEEMS BIG

When we explore *issues, evidence, impact,* and *context* with the client, and mutually conclude that the impact is substantial, a fair question arises: What has stopped the client organization from resolving these issues on its own? What has been tried before and what stopped it from working? If something has stopped the client in the past, it is likely to do so again. We will both be better off discovering and removing the constraints.

THE CONSTRAINTS QUESTION

If the situation has been going on for a while, the constraints question is "What has stopped the organization from successfully resolving these issues before now?" If this is a new opportunity, with no history, the constraints question is "What, if anything, might prevent the successful implementation of this solution going forward?"

> ❖ What has stopped the organization from resolving these issues before now?

The answer to this question can provide valuable insight, yet for some reason it is often not asked. Perhaps, at some level, consultants fear that clients will magically discover that they can do it themselves. If that is the clients' best choice, they will figure it out—usually after we have spent a lot of time and resources giving them a well-thought-out proposal. Let's get real and find out what is going on. The answer to the constraints question falls into two broad categories: good constraints and bad constraints.

GOOD CONSTRAINTS

Good constraints are barriers from the past that no longer exist. Clients did not have a budget before, and now they do. They did not have various approvals, and now they do. It was not a top priority, and now it is. Good constraints are also those things we can do for clients that they cannot do

> ❖ Good constraints: things clients can't do that we can do for them.

for themselves. For instance, clients say they do not have enough time, enough people, enough expertise or know-how, etc. It may not be their core competence or where they want to focus their resources. If so, they have *convinced themselves* of two things:

1. The impact is big.
2. They cannot or will not fix it themselves.

Bad Constraints

Bad constraints are factors that have prevented success in the past and, if not changed, will prevent it again in the future.

For instance:

- Clients have not been able to get this adequately budgeted.
- They cannot get buy-in from the executive committee.
- The XYZ group has a vested interest in killing it.
- Politics always get in the way.
- It has been too complicated.
- They have had higher priorities.

Our question is "What is different this time?" If nothing *is* different, it is likely nothing will *be* different. It is critical to understand what prevented the adoption of the solution in the past, and whether that will prevent it again. Two things are vulnerable: the solution *adoption* (their decision to go with the solution), and the solution *execution*

> ❖ Bad constraints: things that have stopped success in the past, which if uncorrected, will stop it again this time.

(how well we can implement the solution and make it work). *Slow down,* rather than speed up. We might say to the client something like "I have a

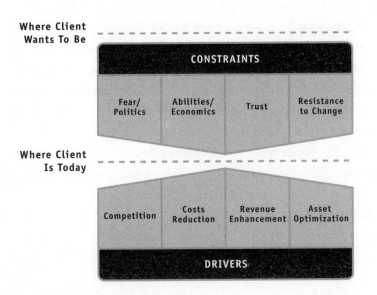

concern. It sounds like even if we come up with the best possible solution, even if it would really get you the results we discussed, it won't be adopted. Politics have killed it in the past and will do so this time too. What do you think we should do?" (see "Yellow Lights" on page 37)

Frequently clients will say some version of "Can *you* help us?" Just as clients will pay you to get important evidence or to quantify the impact, they will pay you to help remove a constraint. Clients know the impact is big, and they know they will not achieve the opportunity unless the constraints are removed. If the constraints cannot be removed, can they be managed or circumvented? If not, do you and the client want to proceed?

Many times, the harder you push on the system, the harder the system pushes back. You often gain more business by identifying and removing constraints than by pushing harder on the reasons to buy.

When the Client Won't Move

> ❖ When you invite clients to move off the solution, either they will move or they won't. If they won't move, it is probably for a reason.

When you invite clients to move off the solution, either they move or they do not. If the client cannot, or will not, move off the solution, that is a yellow light. Slow down, rather than speed up. One of the following may be happening:

1. You are talking with the wrong people. They do not really know the problems and results. You will want to make the case that, in order to get a solution that exactly meets their needs, whether they choose you or not, you will need to talk with the people closely connected to the problems/results. You will not know what to propose if you do not accurately understand what needs to be solved.

2. It is not a real opportunity. They do not want to give you information because they do not really intend to hire you. If you sense this is the case, you may want to gracefully offer to exit. If they want you to stay, they need to give you a good reason. If there is no good reason, this is not where you want to invest your time or company resources.

3. You have been ineffective in your communication. Perhaps you have not given them compelling reason (IQ) to move off the solution;

perhaps you have not created sufficient rapport or safety (EQ) and they do not trust your intent; perhaps the way you moved off the solution was worded poorly and there is a better way to say it.

4. The solution is required by law or regulation. The clients' motivation may be compliance rather than resolution of underlying business problems and results. An example of this would be an outside audit for a public company. In these scenarios, you may need to structure the conversation around criteria for meeting the requirement rather than business issues. (See Eliciting Decision Criteria below.)

5. It is a "predetermined solution." The client, rightly or wrongly, has decided there is an opportunity and has determined what solution the company is going to buy. Allegedly, the client plans to buy it from either you or a competitor. To merely accept the predetermined solution is a risk. If you accept that risk, it will be helpful to structure the conversation around the client's decision criteria—how he or she will decide one solution is better than another, and the criteria for an ideal solution provider.

Eliciting Decision Criteria

When trying to elicit clients' criteria for making a decision, we can structure a conversation around two topics:

1. Their criteria for the ideal implementation.
2. Their criteria for the ideal solution provider.

We could start out with: "Given that you know you're going with Product X, what are your criteria for an ideal implementation of X?" You would elicit a list of criteria (issues) and make sure it was complete. You would explore the evidence and impact of each issue, in order of importance, and investigate context and constraints.

> ❖ "What is most important to you about ____?"

We could also ask, "What will be most important to you, in terms of the people you work with?" We would then proceed to structure a conversation, however loosely, around those criteria as well.

Even though it is challenging to develop evidence and impact for intangible issues, it is still helpful to try. For instance, clients say they want better service: Do they have evidence of poor service in the past or present? What was the impact of getting bad service? In the future, how will they know with certainty they are getting good service? What specific measurements will they use? If no measurements exist, are they important to establish? Would they like some help setting the measurements up? What would be the real payoff to the project and/or company if they got superior service? Who or what else would be affected by good or bad service? What has prevented them from getting excellent service in the past?

The more skillful we are at inviting clients to move off the solution, the more often they will follow our lead. When a client will not move, it is helpful to understand the reason, and act appropriately.

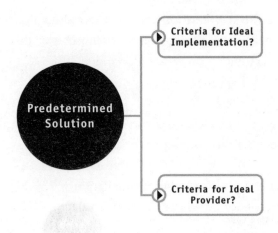

Overview

We have covered a lot of information. Let's step back for a moment and look at the big picture. Remember we are trying to gain mutual understanding around the following:

> **Issues:** What problems or results is the client trying to address? In what priority?
>
> **Evidence:** How do we define the problem? How do we measure success?

Impact: What are the financial and intangible costs and benefits?
Context: Who or what else is affected by the issues and the solution?
Constraints: What has stopped (or might stop) the organization from resolving these issues?

One consistent means of eliciting this information is to structure the conversation:

Move off the solution
Get out all of the issues the solution must address
Prioritize the issues by importance
Gather evidence and impact for issues in order of importance
Explore context and constraints

A structured conversation for a requested solution on supply chain management might look like the accompanying chart:

Structure the Conversation

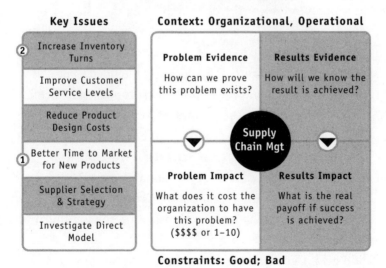

A flow chart of a structured conversation might look like the following:

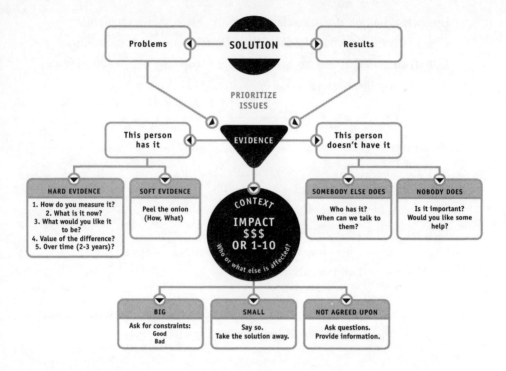

If you wanted to look at the desired information as a list of inquiries, they would be:

1. What are all of the issues the solution is intended to resolve?
2. What's letting you know it's a problem (problem evidence)?
3. What is the impact on the business (problem impact)?
4. How would you measure success (result evidence)?
5. What is the payoff if success is achieved (result impact)?
6. Who or what else is affected (operational context)?
7. What is the big picture (organizational context)?
8. What has stopped the organization from resolving this in the past (constraints)?
9. Did I get it right? Did I leave anything out (summarize)?

In most situations, if the Opportunity is not qualified, nothing else matters. Asking effective questions adds value and insight to the client as well as providing needed information to you.

CHAPTER FOUR

QUALIFYING RESOURCES

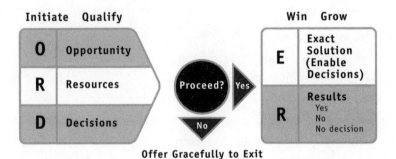

Even if there is a qualified Opportunity, you cannot help someone succeed who cannot or will not commit sufficient resources to manifest the opportunity. Three critical resources to examine are: *time, people,* and *money.*

In qualifying, the discussion of resources need not be lengthy and detailed. We want to know if there is an overlap between what clients feel is necessary and available, and what we feel is required, in order to get a solution that meets their needs. If there are yellow lights, we want to confront them early and not late in the process.

> ❖ You cannot help someone succeed without sufficient time, people, and money.

TIME

We have just gone through the Opportunity with the client, and have mutually agreed it is worth achieving. A good timetable question is "What is the date by which you hope to have these results in place?" Or we might ask, "When were you hoping to get started?" or "What kind of time frame are we working with?" The timing question is not hard to ask—you just have to ask it.

> ❖ When do they want to have the results in place? When were they hoping to get started?

We are not pushing for commitment or trying to "close the deal." We are just finding out what works for them and, in doing so, ensuring that we and the client are on the same page. Yellow lights on timing include:

1. The timing is too soon.
2. The timing is too far into the future.
3. The timing is undefined.

Yellow lights in timing are usually at the extremes (too soon or too far off), and they are predictable. For example, if timing is too far off, we might say, "I'm confused. You said this was costing you $10 million a year, yet you want to wait three years to fix it. That's $30 million lost forever. What makes that acceptable?" We can only say something like that if we have done a good job in Opportunity. Otherwise, we will not know the financial assumptions, and we will not have developed the rapport to challenge their assumption.

What if the yellow light is that they want it too soon—faster than we can realistically perform? It is helpful to find out *what is driving that date.* There may be political, financial, or organizational circumstances unrelated to the project time line that we can help meet without compromising timely delivery. Perhaps we have options to break the initiative into phases and prioritize what should come first. However, if they truly need it faster than we can deliver, it is a yellow light. We may choose to say, "I have a concern. I think it's possible for you to get the results we talked about; I don't think it's possible within that time period. If we could actually get you the results, yet take three months instead of two weeks, should we keep talking?" We will find out either that the time constraint is real (and at least you found the red light early on), or that there are options to address the client's concerns without compromising the solution.

PEOPLE

We would like to know how the client anticipates dividing effort and responsibilities between his or her company and ours.

This is at a high level; we are not trying to get into the specific details or daily activities. We want a rough sense that the division of labor fits our and the client's criteria for success. Additionally, if there are people from the client's company who are critical to executing the solution, we want to make sure the client intends to make them available. We are looking for yellow lights; as with timing, when they are present they are at the extremes—either the client wants too little of their people's involvement or too much of their involvement.

> ❖ Who does what? Which people are critical for success?

Too little of their involvement

A potential concern is that the client may not give us access to the key people we need to be successful. For example, if top management's involvement is critical, yet the client is saying that is problematic, we want to test the yellow light early rather than later: "I have a concern. In our experience, unless we can get participation by top management, it is highly unlikely you will get the results you want. What would have to happen to make sure we get their participation?"

Too much of their involvement

If clients want to do critical parts of the initiative themselves, we may be concerned that they will not commit the necessary time, quality, or expertise. This is particularly important if our performance depends on them doing a good job. If we perceive a yellow light in this regard, it may require both courage and consideration in testing it. Suggesting to clients, explicitly or implicitly, that their people cannot or will not do a good job is not the easiest message to communicate. One option is to say something along the lines of "Help me understand how you view the responsibility for this project. Are you hoping that we will manage the project and take responsibility for successful completion—and that you will essentially subcontract your people to us? Or are you going to be fully responsible for management and results, and subcontract us?" If they want us to take responsibility, they would certainly expect us to replace any of our people if they were not producing timely, quality results. We will want the authority to manage their people as we would manage our own people. Anybody who is not putting in the time or producing the quality we expect can be taken off the project and replaced with someone more capable—either from their company or ours.

MONEY

Money is typically a function of scope, timing, and division of labor. We have talked about scope in terms of the results the client wants to achieve (Opportunity). We have talked about timing and division of labor. At this point, it is logical to talk about money. However, just because it is logical does not mean it is not emotional. It always seems that the energy level picks up when we finally start talking with the client about money.

There are two times it is beneficial to talk about money: One is at this point, in Resources, and the other is later, in Exact Solution/Enabling Decisions. In Resources, we are talking only about *value* justification. We are not going to give clients our fees or price, and we are not asking them for the specific dollars they have in a budget. We are trying to understand if there is congruence between what they think it is *worth* to get the desired results (the return), and what we think is *necessary* to produce those results (the investment). In the Exact Solution step, when we actually present our proposal and give them a price, *price* negotiation may come into play.

The client's question, "Are we getting the best deal?" (price negotiation)

is very different from "Can we afford
this?" (value justification); it is important to understand the difference. Here
is an example. Let's say you are looking

> ❖ How much are they willing to invest
> to get their desired results?

to buy a new car. One of the first economic decisions you make is the dollar range you can afford to spend on a car. When you actually go into the
marketplace, your price range may shift, but fundamentally you have some
notion of the worth of a vehicle to you. Let's say you decide you can spend
$30,000–$35,000. You find the vehicle you really want and it costs $33,000.
Now what do you do? You bargain! The issue is not whether you can afford
to spend $33,000; you have already figured that out. The issue is whether
you are getting the best deal. In Resources, all we are trying to find out
from clients is their beliefs about worth and about value. What amount of
investment seems reasonable for the returns they expect?

Remember, intent counts more than technique. Our intent is to figure
out if we and the client are headed in the same direction and whether we
should keep going. If not, let's find out now, so we do not waste each
other's time. There is a price below which people would not reasonably expect to get good quality; there is a price above which any additional features and benefits, no matter how impressive, would not make a difference.
The client has a range. It may not be explicit or conscious, but it is there.
We have a range too. The question is whether our ranges overlap. If not, we
probably cannot do business.

The authors have seen consultants who have spent more money to develop and present a proposal than the clients had in their budget for the
solution itself. The consultants never knew it was happening until they
presented their proposal to the client. They could have found out in two
minutes and did not find out for many months.

If you walk out of qualifying meetings with clients and do not know
how much they are thinking of spending, and they do not know how
much you are thinking of charging, you will both be guessing. This is mutual mystification. No guessing! The first time you test price with the client
should not be when you present your proposal. Guessing is not only unnecessary, it is costly.

So, when do we talk about money?

- **After Opportunity:** after we have quantified the impact.
- **Before Exact Solution/Enabling Decisions:** before we present our solution with its price to the client.
- **At the Right Place in Decisions:** with the person(s) most appropriate in the decision process.

Our goal in qualifying: Are we and the client thinking along the same lines?

Key Question: Are we in the same ballpark?

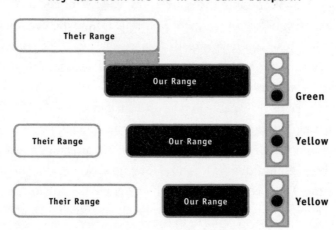

How Do We Talk about Money?

Here are two good choices for initiating conversation about money:

1. "Have you thought about what level of investment is appropriate for the results we've discussed?"
2. "Have you established a budget for this project?" (Or "for this purchase.")

There are some predictable responses to the money question:

"Yes." (And they can't/won't share it with us.)
"Yes." (And it seems sufficient.)

"Yes." (And it's too small.)

"Yes." (And it's too big—we wish!)

"No, we haven't."

"You tell me how much it will cost."

"Money's no problem."

"If it's worth it, we'll come up with the money" or, "It has to be self-funding."

"I don't know." (Someone else knows or no one knows.)

Because these responses are finite and predictable, we should have some predictable responses ready.

The "Three-Part Response"

Here is a good response that works in most cases:

> Part 1: "I don't know how much this will cost you. Every client situation is unique.
> Part 2: However, other companies in similar situations, successfully achieving the results we've been talking about, tend to invest between X and Y.
> Part 3: Can you see yourself falling somewhere in that range?"

Notice we have not said, "We charge other companies. . . ." We are merely saying that other companies in similar situations who were successful in achieving these results—whether with us, with a competitor, or by themselves—invested between X and Y. Y should be no more than 25 to 50 percent more than X—for example, between $200,000 to $250,000. A range between $100,000 and $10,000,000, is not a meaningful range.

When we ask them, "Can you see yourself somewhere in that range?" we usually get one of two responses:

1. "Yes" (however grudging).
2. "Oh, my goodness, that's way more than we were thinking." (It goes without saying, this is a yellow light.)

We just want to find out if our ranges overlap. If the client falls out of the chair, turns white, or starts screaming or crying, we may have a problem. We should pick up on these subtle cues. It is better to deal with these yellow lights now than after we have committed a lot of our company's resources to a proposal that will not make sense to the client.

During our initial conversations with the client, we may not have a realistic range in mind; we may not want to give out a number without further input from our colleagues. If so, we can get the client's permission for the following: we will go back and work with our team a bit; we can then get a sense for where the proposal might head economically, and call the client back for guidance. When we call clients back with a range, they can tell us to either keep working, or to stop the presses because we are thinking of two radically different price ranges. All we are going to do with our team at this stage is run some rough numbers. We are not going to have everybody run around and develop a big proposal when we have no idea what the client is willing to invest.

Here are some examples of how the three-part response is applied.

"No. We Don't Have a Budget."

We might respond with questions like "What were your expectations? " or "How do you typically fund projects like this?"

We could also go with the three-part response: "Let's bat around some numbers so you have something to work with. At this point:

1. I don't know how much this will cost you. Every client situation is unique.
2. However, other companies in similar situations—successfully achieving the results we've been talking about—tend to invest between X and Y.
3. Can you see yourself falling somewhere in that range?"

"You Tell Me."

The client says some version of "You're the expert. You tell me how much this will cost."

We might say, "Fair enough. At this point:

1. I don't know how much this will cost you. Every client situation is unique.
2. However, other companies in similar situations—successfully achieving the results we've been talking about—tend to invest between X and Y.
3. Can you see yourself falling somewhere in that range?"

"Money's No Problem."

What if they say, "Oh, money's not an issue. Just give us a proposal, prove that it's worth it, and we'll come up with the money." The three-part response will serve us well again.

We might say, "Well that's good to hear. Just so there are no surprises, at this point:

1. I don't know how much this will cost you. Every client situation is unique.
2. However, other companies in similar situations—successfully achieving the results we've been talking about—tend to invest between X and Y.
3. Can you see yourself falling somewhere in that range?"

By the way, money is *always* an issue.

"I Can't Tell You."

The client might say, "I'd rather not tell you the number we have in mind," or "I'm not allowed disclose a figure; that's against our policy."

We might say, "That's not a problem. I don't want you to do anything you're not comfortable with. I don't really need a specific number. Let *me* throw out some figures and get your reaction." At this point you can continue using the same three listed responses/questions we used when money was no object.

"I Don't Know."

The client might give us some version of "I don't know." It is then fair to ask, "That's not a problem. Who would know?" Even when we find out who else we need to talk to, we can still try out the three-part response on this person and get a preliminary reaction.

"How Did You Come Up with That Number?"

Either we have an overlap in ranges, or we are left with one of two situations: They have a budget and it's too small; or, we give them a range and they do not fit into it. For whatever reason, their expected expenditure is less than what we feel it needs to be. Whenever the client comes up with a number that is smaller than our number, it is helpful to ask, "And how did you come up with that number?"

This is an important question. The response often falls into one of two categories: logistics or value. You do not want to discuss *value* if the reason is logistics, and you do not want to explore *logistics* if the reason is value. The way we find the answer is by asking, "And how did you come up with that number?"

When they are NOT in your range:

They have a range or number in their head

What is it?

Logistics ◄ **How did they arrive at that number?** ► **Value**

Logistics or Value?

A logistics issue would be something like "That's all we have left in this year's budget." At that point, we want to find out what that number is, and how much they have in *next* year's budget. They are not saying the investment it is not worth it; they are merely saying they have some logistical constraints.

They may also say, "That's all I'm authorized to spend." Our response could then be "That's fine. Who is authorized to spend the larger amount?" Or they may say, "That's all we have to get started." We might respond, "Great. Let's say we get started and are successful—where would the rest of the funding come from?" The client is not arguing about the value of doing it; he or she is concerned about the logistics.

Value, on the other hand, involves some version of "That's all we think it's worth." We clearly have a yellow light, so we may as well deal with it. We could say, "Well, I appreciate your sharing that information. We may have a problem. I believe it's possible to get you the results you're talking about, but I don't think it's possible for less than $250,000 to $300,000. What do you feel we should do? (Or, "Give me some guidance; does that mean you would not want us to give you a proposal?")

If they say a version of "Yes, we still want you to give us a proposal," then we are getting mixed signals and we state it: "I'm confused. It sounds to me that even if we came in with the best possible solution and you were convinced this was better than anything else you could do, you wouldn't buy it because your budget is less than what we feel is necessary to get the results. It doesn't seem to be a good use of time to prepare a proposal that won't be accepted." The client then has an opportunity to either turn the yellow light to green and convince us that money is available for the right solution, or turn the light to red.

If the client says, "Don't bother doing a proposal if that's the price you'll come in with." The client is on the brink of turning the yellow light to red. It's helpful to remember where we are in the process. The value of the solution to the

> ❖ It is usually not a question of money, it is a question of belief.

client is much higher than the investment numbers we are putting out; otherwise, we would not be at this point. We would have had a yellow light in Opportunity. *It is usually not a question of money; it's a question of beliefs*—typically one of three beliefs:

1. The client does not believe in the *value* of the solution.
2. They do not believe that *what we do* will give them that value.
3. They believe they can get the same value *somewhere else for less.*

It is useful to uncover the belief that is stopping them from doing something that seems to make sense. So we say, "Frank, usually when we get to this point in the conversation, and we're so far apart on the value of doing this, I find one of three things is happening. Either:

- you don't believe in the value we discussed,
- you don't believe that what we do will provide that value,
- you believe you can get the same value somewhere else for less.

"Is one of those three things happening?"

If the client does not really believe the numbers we developed in the Opportunity discussion, we might say, "Well, if I didn't have confidence in the return, I'd question the investment myself. Let's revisit our numbers and see what you think is more realistic."

If they have some reason to doubt that what we do will give them the desired results, we say, "I'm glad you're willing to say so. If I had doubts, I'd probably question *any* investment. Let's talk about your concerns."

If they have reason to believe they can get the same results somewhere else for less, then let's get real—they should. If they didn't do it, they would be fiscally irresponsible. Their only doubt would be whether they really are going to get the same results. Is it an apples-to-apples comparison? We should make sure it is.

Here is a possible approach:

> CLIENT: I think I can get the same results for less money.
> CONSULTANT: If you can, you should. If I were in your shoes, and I could get exactly the same results for less money, I'd be fiscally irresponsible not to do it. I respect that. I guess the only way you could get burned is if you were not really comparing apples to apples. Do you have a proposal from someone else?
> CLIENT: Yes.
> CONSULTANT: I'll tell you what I'd be willing to do. I'll invest a half-hour of my time to go over the proposal together. I don't want you

to show me anything proprietary. I just want to get an idea of the scope—what they say they are going to do and what results they will produce. If what they are going to do is the same as what we have in mind, I'll advise you to go with them. If I see some radical differences, I'll point them out. You might still go with them. At least you will be making a well-informed decision. Does that sound reasonable?

If clients do not have a proposal, we can inquire how they came up with their belief. If they say they are going to get a proposal, we can say, "Great. When you get the proposal, I'd be willing to invest . . . ," and we offer the same suggestion as stated earlier.

If they ask us to just send in our proposal and say they will judge it on its merits, we have a decision. It does not make a lot of sense to send in a proposal that seems doomed to failure. We might say something like, "Susan, if I hear you right, you believe that someone else can deliver the same results we can for less money. It doesn't seem you need a proposal from us. I'd be happy to offer one if we can come up with some compelling reasons why it would be in your company's best interests to spend more money with us than with another party. We would still have to prove to your satisfaction that we could deliver on that difference. However, if we can't come up with a difference that makes a difference, it seems like we'd be wasting both our companies' time. What's your sense?"

If we can't resolve the client's underlying beliefs about value, something has to change or our yellow light is about to turn red. Perhaps we can negotiate changes in scope, timing, or division of labor that would achieve the desired price. Perhaps other key stakeholders have different views on value justification and we can enlist their help. Perhaps we can be more creative with our business model or deal structure. Or perhaps this is an unqualified deal and we are fortunate to find out early rather than late.

Review

A graphical representation of the money conversation is shown in the flow chart that follows.

**Have you thought about what amount of investment
is appropriate for the results we discussed?**

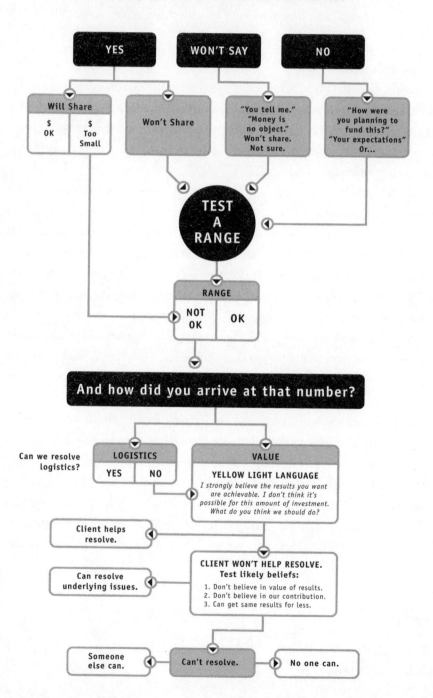

Remember, our intent is to get a solution that exactly meets the client's needs. It is impossible to take fiscal realities out of that analysis. If we come back with a solution that is ten times what our clients can afford, we have not helped them, or ourselves. If the first time we try out an investment amount is when they hear our presentation or read our proposal, we are guessing. And the cost of guessing can be very high.

Don't go into the Exact Solution step without qualifying the client on time, people, and money. Especially money! No guessing.

CHAPTER FIVE

QUALIFYING DECISIONS

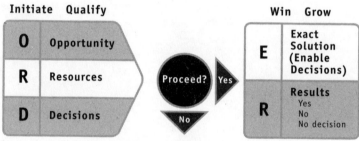

Smart people, trying to do good things, can make bad decisions. Dr. Paul Nutt, author of *Why Decisions Fail*, investigated the success rate of decisions made by executives and managers at 356 companies. *More than 50 percent of all decisions failed,* either because they were quickly abandoned, only partially implemented, or never adopted at all.

When companies are set up to make bad decisions, and we acquiesce and participate, we suffer. Our sales cycles lengthen. We spend considerable time on activities that don't provide value to anyone; this raises our costs and is demoralizing, if not downright demeaning. We work diligently on opportunities where *no one* gets awarded the business. Clients deny us information and access to key stakeholders; we have to guess about important criteria and concerns, and we often guess wrong. We make elaborate presentations to people who cannot or will not make a decision. We fail to get our ideas in front of the people who could most appreciate and best take advantage of them. Our win rate goes down and our dissatisfaction goes up.

Understanding and influencing how decisions are made is a critical juncture in the sales journey. During the entire sales process, this is our greatest opportunity to reduce frustration and help actualize profitable results. It is a big deal. We can reduce the agony of failure and help our clients, and ourselves, actually make money.

Only a small percentage of consultants do a good job of articulating and guiding the decision process. Fewer still gain access to all the key stakeholders, deeply understand what is important to them, and accurately elicit their criteria for making the decisions at hand. The few of us who do it well will be highly regarded and richly rewarded by clients, and will distance ourselves from the competition.

To improve our success in this pivotal sphere we will develop three key abilities: articulating and influencing the decision process; gaining access to key stakeholders; and understanding decision criteria.

ARTICULATING AND INFLUENCING THE DECISION PROCESS

We are unlikely to find something if we don't know what we are looking for. Imagine for a moment that you have a client who will tell you honestly and accurately *anything* you want to know about the company's decision process. What would you want to know? Here are some common responses from consultants:

- Who is going to make the decision?
- Who is going to influence the decision?
- Who can veto the decision?
- Who signs the check?
- Who approves the decision?
- What are the criteria for a "yes" decision?
- What is the process?
- How will the decision be made?

- What information do you need?
- When are you going to make the decision?
- Who is the competition?
- How do I stack up against the competition?
- What do I have to do to win?
- Are you sure you'll go with *someone*?

That's a lot to find out. Having a structure and sequence of questions for eliciting this information greatly increases our likelihood of getting it. Here is an approach that works well.

First, find out the *steps* involved in making the decision. Next, find out what *decision* gets made in each step. (Sometimes these two are the same, and sometimes they are different.) Find out *when* they will decide. Find out *who* is involved in each step. Finally, find out *how* each person will decide. To find out how each person will decide, talk with them personally. One of the key outcomes in this process is to *find out the "how" directly from the "who."*

When we talk to the "who," we will explore the Opportunity from their perspective—as well as their *criteria* for making the decision. Those criteria will include how they will decide between *alternative solutions* (the competition). We also want to know their criteria for a good presentation—what they want us to address that will allow them to make a good, well-informed decision.

The authors call collecting this information "working the grid."

The Decision Process

Steps	Decision	When	Who	Criteria/ Beliefs
What are all of the steps?	What decision gets made in each step?	When will they decide?	Who is involved in each step	How will each decision maker decide?

Competition:	How will they decide between alternative solutions?
Gain/Loss:	Who in the organization stands to win or lose if this solution is adopted?
Personal Stake:	How does the person we are talking with win or lose?

The Steps

A helpful initial question is "What are the steps you need to take as an organization, to make a confident yes or no decision?" We are looking for a discrete series of go/no-go events that culminate in a final yes or no decision.

There are three reasons to start with these steps rather than ask, "Who is going to make this decision?" First, by asking such a question, it may imply to those with whom we are talking that they are not important. Second, any given person is likely to answer the question by saying, "I am," even if that is only partially correct. Third, if clients do not have a clear picture of what the steps are, they are unlikely to give us complete and accurate information about all the people involved in the decision. The steps may not be well formed in their minds; they may omit or collapse steps; they may talk only about the first step, or perhaps the last step.

When the steps are completed, they should allow the client to feel completely confident in saying *either* yes or no. To get good information about the steps, we need to allow the responses of yes and no to be equal choices—and it sometimes helps to emphasize that *"No is okay."* When people genuinely feel that no is an acceptable answer, they will give us better information. As soon as they feel we are trying to pin them down and lead them to our conclusion, the trust alarm goes off and we get resistance rather than cooperation. It might sound like this: "We've talked about what you want to accomplish and the resources available to make it happen. What are the steps you will need to take as an organization to feel comfortable and confident saying either 'Yes, this makes sense, let's do it,' or 'No, now that we've explored it, we feel we have better uses for our resources'?" If we are fairly confident they will actually select a solution provider we might inquire, "It sounds like getting the results we discussed is critical for your company. What are the steps you'll need to take as an organization to feel confident that whatever choice you make is the right decision?"

Remember: If you want good information about what it takes to get a yes, make no be okay.

The steps might look something like the chart below.

DECISION PROCESS EXAMPLE				
Steps	Decision	When	Who	Criteria/Beliefs
Talk to 6-8 Companies				
Narrow to 3				
Pass on to Selection Committee				
Refer to CEO				

Articulating the steps is one goal. Influencing them is another. After determining the steps as accurately as we can, we examine them from two points of view: First, if *clients* follow this path, will *they* make a good decision? Second, if *we* follow this path, will it serve *us* well?

If we have thought through an "ideal" set of steps, we can often suggest what we see as improvements. Perhaps steps are omitted or can be streamlined. Perhaps the client would be better served by changing the order in which things happen. Perhaps we can offer a different way of proceeding altogether.

Mahan was coaching a consultant on a several hundred million dollar opportunity. A large determinant in winning the deal was gaining acceptance from the buying organization to switch two of the steps in the decision process. The buyer planned to have operations personnel decide on which technology solution they preferred to use and then make a recommendation to the executive committee. Mahan's client was proposing a solution that fundamentally changed how the buyer did its business; it included a good deal of process change along with new technology. The consultant acknowledged that his top competitor was likely to win the deal if the decision was based primarily on technology alone; the competitor had more mature technology and stronger relationships with people in operations while Mahan's client had stronger relationships at the executive level.

His client advocated to the buyer that the decision should go first to the executive committee to decide on what would best serve the objectives of the business, and then to operations to assure that they could work effectively with the preferred solution provider's technology. The argument was essentially to let the needs of the business drive the technology choice rather than letting the technology choice determine the needs of the business.

The buyer agreed. Mahan's client won exceptional acceptance at the executive level. Several key executives then helped gain the cooperation and buy-in from operations. The people Mahan coached were convinced that if these two steps had not been reversed, they well may have lost rather than won this deal—one which has worked well for all parties.

The Decisions

In the decision grid example pictured earlier, there were four steps:

1. We're going to talk to maybe six to eight companies.
2. We're going to narrow those down to three companies.
3. We're going to pass those three on to our selection committee.
4. We might refer it up to the CEO just to get her blessing.

In each of the steps, we want to be absolutely clear about what decision gets made. Sometimes the way the "step" is worded makes the decision obvious. It is clear what the second decision is: Which three of the six to eight companies will get further consideration? However, the other decisions are not clear. For instance, when three companies are "passed on" to the selection committee," what recommendation is made? Is it "We picked three companies for you to interview; here you go"? Is it "Here are the pros and cons of the three; you decide"? Is it "Here is the one we recommend, and here is our justification"? Or is it something else?

Also, if they *might* "refer it up to the CEO," what determines if they will or they won't? What decision really gets made at that step? Does the CEO just rubber-stamp the committee's decision, or does she really look to make the decision herself? Our goal is to clearly understand what specifically these people decide or influence in each step.

Our decision grid example might fill out as shown here.

DECISION PROCESS EXAMPLE				
Steps	Decision	When	Who	Criteria/Beliefs
Talk to 6–8 Companies	Which 6–8?			
Narrow to 3	Which 3? Defend choices			
Pass on to Selection Committee	Recommend top choice and defend			
Refer to CEO	Confirm or push back			

The When

Each go/no-go decision should have at least a target date on it. This becomes a manageable, if flexible, "up-front agreement" between us and the client. We certainly will not be surprised if things change; we anticipate the grid will be modified as we talk to other stakeholders. If we remain explicit about the changes, we will definitely shorten our business-development cycle. If time lines are missing or fuzzy, suggest some. Choose milestones that would seem reasonable to you if you were the client.

Our continuing example might look as shown here.

DECISION PROCESS EXAMPLE				
Steps	Decision	When	Who	Criteria/Beliefs
Talk to 6–8 Companies	Which 6–8?	May 15–June 1		
Narrow to 3	Which 3? Defend choices	June 8		
Pass on to Selection Committee	Recommend top choice and defend	June 15		
Refer to CEO	Confirm or push back	June 22–26		

If the decision process seems unduly long, we now have two possible challenges. First, in Opportunity, we developed an economic value of the business issues; let's say it was $10 million a year. A six-month decision process could cost the client $5 million. The client is unlikely to save that much in a competitive bidding process. Second, as seen in Resources, there is a time by which clients want the results in place. Does the length of the decision process jeopardize this objective? If so, what creative options can the client pursue?

The Who

We have three columns in the chart completed now: the steps, what decisions get made in those steps, and when those decisions will be made. The fourth question we ask our client is "*Who* is involved in each step?"

At this point, we are not asking what each person's role is, or the reasons each is involved in this step. We are going to talk to those people directly and find out what they do and how they see things. Later on, based on our direct conversations, we can state our understanding of each person's role.

Some typical roles would be:

- **Initiator:** Opens the transaction.
- **Gatekeeper:** Controls information flow and access.
- **Champion:** Willing to support our cause and aid access to decision makers.
- **Influencer:** Nonbuyer who affects the purchase—from inside or outside the organization.
- **User:** Affected directly by the purchase.
- **Decision maker:** Makes the decision to buy.
- **Ratifier:** Approves the decision to buy.

People often take on multiple roles in the decision process. In complex opportunities, it is almost always helpful to have an organizational chart—either a formal one or an ad hoc one—created with the client. Many organizations find it helpful to use software or other tools to map and manage the network of interrelationships.

Our ongoing decision grid example might now look as shown here.

DECISION PROCESS EXAMPLE				
Steps	Decision	When	Who	Criteria/Beliefs
Talk to 6–8 Companies	Which 6–8?	May 15–June 1	Me	
Narrow to 3	Which 3? Defend choices	June 8	Me, End User, 1 Unit Head	
Pass on to Selection Committee	Recommend top choice and defend	June 15	CFO, CIO, SVP, 4 Unit Heads	
Refer to CEO	Confirm or push back	June 22–26	CEO	

Ratifier or Closet Decision Maker?

One of the most difficult things to discern is whether a particular key stakeholder is a ratifier or a decision maker. For example, if the CEO is actually a ratifier, we do not need to see her. She is probably just going to rubber-stamp the decisions. The *real* decision makers are going to be on the selection committee. If the CEO *is* going to make the final decision, we need to see her, or we will be guessing both about how she sees the solution and her criteria for deciding. It's often hard to decide which role a person is assuming, and a wrong decision can be problematic.

The authors were working with a potential client that was trying to decide between a well-known competitor and our company. The paradigm of the competitor was "Start at the top; stay at the top." They would talk only to the executive vice president. It turned out that the EVP had a higher *organizational* role but a subordinate *buying* role—he had delegated the buying decision to somebody else. The person who had the buying decision was ignored by the competitor's people and did not feel respected by them. It certainly influenced her decision to choose us instead. The lesson is: do not confuse organizational authority with buying authority. In today's world they do not always equate.

In a different situation, one of our competitors' paradigms was "Get to the economic buyer." The competitor misjudged a companywide executive group as the "economic buyer." The authors could understand the confusion; we could not figure out whether the selection committee or the executive group was the real decision maker. We decided to keep working with the selection committee without interviewing the executives. The competitor decided to withdraw when it could not meet with the executive group.

Now instead of three competitors there were only two. It turned out that the executive group members were ratifiers and not decision makers. We talked with every member on the selection committee before our presentation and won the business. We made a gut call and it served us well. We could have also invested a lot of time with the selection committee only to have the executive group stall or counteract the decision.

To answer the question "Decision maker or ratifier?" it is helpful to ask, "Of the last ten times you sent a recommendation to X, how many times did he or she go against it or pass it back for more scrutiny?" If the answer is "Four or five," then X is a decision maker and we should talk with that person. If the answer is "Maybe one, if ever," then X is probably a ratifier, and we do not need to burn political capital to see him or her.

Did We Get All of the Who?

Have you ever walked into a presentation feeling well prepared, only to have a person you have never heard of or met enter the room and express strong opinions about how the decision should be made? Perhaps the person dismisses your product or service without the benefit of any previous conversations with either you or the other stakeholders. This is not a welcome surprise.

As you talk with the various stakeholders, keep asking who *they* feel you should be talking to. In your Opportunity discussions, listen closely to what the client says about context (Who or what else is affected?) and constraints (What has stopped the organization from resolving these issues on its own?). If you feel there are key stakeholders who are critical to the decision process and whom have not been mentioned, bring up their names or functions and get a reaction. If these are people who are going to make or influence the decision, we would like to talk with them before they do.

GAINING ACCESS TO KEY STAKEHOLDERS

In an ideal world, it is better for clients and stakeholders to talk. It is difficult, if not impossible, for us to exactly meet the needs of people with whom we have never talked. For clients, how we "sell" is a free sample of how we solve. They get to see how we analyze a business opportunity and how we work with them. Yet the world is not ideal. Buyers often have past experiences in which they were abused by either manipulative or inept consultants. As a result, many buyers would rather have a "less than optimal" solution than be aggravated by ignorant, arrogant, or incompetent salespeople. The norm for buyers in relationship to sellers is often "Don't let them get to me; don't let them waste my time."

> ❖ It is difficult, if not impossible, to exactly meet the needs of people with whom we have not talked.

Don't Ask—Advocate

Don't bother asking, "Can I see the people who will be making the decision?" The answer is almost always no. It may or may not be accompanied by a reason. It's like walking into a retail store and the clerk says, "Hello, can I help you?" and we respond, "No, thanks, just looking." It's automatic.

Rather than asking at this point, we advocate, and say something like "Our goal is to come up with a solution that precisely addresses your needs. From what you described to me, these people are key owners of those needs. To make any kind of intelligent proposal, I'll need to talk with them. You know the company better than I do. How do we set that up?"

Reciprocity—The Equivalence of Actions

Clients ask us to spend considerable resources on developing and presenting a solution. The assumption is that the effort we put in will be of value to them. All we are asking of them is a value exchange. We will happily put in the time to develop and present our ideas—even with no guarantee of winning—as long as they will give us access to the information necessary to make those ideas relevant and meaningful. If we are willing to put in *a lot* of time in diagnosis and prescription, are the individuals on their side willing to invest *a little* time (about thirty minutes each) in mutually understanding their priorities?

> ❖ All we are asking for is about 30 minutes of each person's time. If necessary we can do it on the phone.

Yellow Lights

If the client will not let us talk to the key stakeholders, refuses any equivalence of actions, or wants us to spend a lot of time and money merely guessing—that is a strong yellow light. Guessing does not serve the client. If there are several clients involved in the decision, they each bring a unique perspective to the problems, results, evidence, impact, constraints, etc. If we have to guess about their differing beliefs and criteria, we are significantly less likely to give them a proposal that makes sense and is on target. Clients certainly will not get our best analysis. They will have worse rather than better choices available, and they are less likely to make appropriate decisions. Guessing might even needlessly kill the initiative. All we are asking for is about thirty minutes with each key stakeholder; if necessary we can do it over the phone. Isn't that reasonable?

Predictable Responses

If we advocate well, clients will grant access a reasonable percentage of the time. At other times they will give some predictable negative responses. Do these sound familiar?

- "They are too busy. They don't have the time."
- "They asked me to do it. It's my job."
- "You don't need to see them. I can fill you in."
- "It's all in the RFP."
- "They don't see consultants" (or other lower life-forms).

- "It wouldn't be fair to others. We need to keep a level playing field."
- "It's not allowed. It's against our policy."
- "Put your questions in writing. We'll share the answers with everyone."

You could add to the list, yet it is reasonably finite. Because the list is predictable, we can prepare some intelligent replies that will improve our probability of gaining access.

As we construct our replies, remember that intent counts more than technique. Our intent is to get a solution that exactly meets clients' needs. We are going to pursue only two lines of inquiry when we meet with the people we're trying to see: we need to know the *Opportunity* from their perspective, and we need to know their *criteria* for making the decision. We are only asking for about thirty minutes with each of them, and, if necessary, we are willing to do it over the phone.

Match and Lead

There is a communication tool called "match and lead," which is founded on the idea that if you cannot meet people where they are, you do not have the right or ability to lead them somewhere else. Milton Erickson, a famous hypnotherapist, was a master of this method. He was brilliant at his craft. Erickson started with whatever was presented by clients; he never resisted or tried to change their starting point. He precisely matched them where they were before he offered choices of where to go next. For example, if someone said, "You can't hypnotize me!" he might say, "You're right. There is no way I could hypnotize you! There is no way you could fall, gently, into a light, relaxing, trance." With his voice getting softer, he might continue, "There is no way you could begin to relax, to soften your focus; to ease your mind, relaxing, in your own

> ❖ If you cannot meet people where they are, you have not earned the right or ability to lead them someplace new.

comfortable way, gently. . . ." Before they knew it, people were in a trance state, something they had just said would be impossible.

Although we may not be Milton Ericksons, we can, as professional communicators, use the basics of match and lead. We can genuinely get on the same side of the table as our counterparts. We can understand where they are coming from. We may have been in the same position ourselves. While we may not agree with them, we can understand them and respect the reasons for their position.

One choice is to see if the reason for *not* granting access can become the reason *for* granting access. For instance, if "time" is the reason for *not* granting access, can "time" be the reason *for* granting access? Here's an example:

> ❖ Can the reason for *not* granting access become the reason *for* granting access?

GATEKEEPER: They are too busy. You can't see them.

CONSULTANT: (Match) "I can appreciate how busy they must be, particularly with all that's going on. I'm sure the last thing they would want is for us to waste their time.

(Lead): And that's my concern. If we get them all in a room and give them a presentation that's not really relevant, or doesn't adequately address their differing perspectives, concerns, or criteria, it will be a huge waste of their time, and they'll hate it. So let's not waste their time.

I will need only about thirty minutes with each of them individually. If necessary, I can do it over the phone. That way we can make the best use of their time during the meeting. You know these people better than I do. What would be the best way for us to set that up?

The language offered in this book is comfortable and compatible with the authors, and has been received well by clients. For others, the same language would not be a fit. If you understand the intent, the technique, and the rationale for responding to predictable gatekeeper objections, you can create your own language.

Following are some more client reasons for not granting access to key stakeholders, along with some reasons why it actually would be in their best interest to allow it.

Fairness

They may say, "It's not fair for you to see them. If we let you do it, we have to do it for everybody." If "fairness" is the reason for *not* doing it, can "fairness" be the reason *for* doing it?

We can certainly understand the clients' desire to be fair—and we appreciate it because we want to be treated fairly. However their ultimate goal is not fairness to outside vendors. The goal (and their fiduciary responsibility) is to be fair to the shareholders and stakeholders of their company, and to be fair to a solution that meets their needs. It would not be fair to expect that we could produce a solution that addresses the priorities of key stakeholders without ever talking to them about those priorities. One should doubt the professionalism and intellectual thoroughness of consultants who feel they can give a prescription without good diagnosis.

Consultants often spend dozens to hundreds to thousands of person-hours developing and preparing to present a solution. We do so with no guarantee we will gain the client's business. And we are willing to do so. All we ask in return is about thirty minutes with each of the key stakeholders so our time will be well spent in coming up with a meaningful solution. Isn't that a fair request?

> ❖ We want to be fair to the client stakeholders and develop a solution that exactly meets their needs. It isn't fair to expect we could do that without talking with them.

We can challenge the idea that if *we* talk to the key stakeholders, all competitors need to as well. Our competitors may not ask to speak to the stakeholders. In the spirit of fairness, we might suggest to clients that they grant access only to those who feel it is imperative. If they don't need to, they won't ask. If they don't ask, the client needn't grant access. That's fair.

Another option is for us to suggest to clients that they let each consultant company spend as little or as much time as it needs with key stakeholders. The client can tell the consultants that a large part of the decision of who to hire will be based on how well the consultants use the clients' time during the interviews; those consultants who waste client time are unlikely to be hired—in fact, they may be eliminated very quickly. Since how consultants sell is a free sample of how they solve, it is better for the client to find out early, rather than late, what each consultant is like to work with.

"I'll Do It for You."

When someone other than us interviews key client stakeholders, there are two big challenges:

1. There will *always* be a dilution of information and meaning. It is unavoidable. We will only get a portion of what was conveyed and will lack what was communicated nonverbally.

2. Clients interveiwing people from their own company will not ask the questions we would. They may not ask any questions at all; they might just report what they were told. If they are interviewing superiors, they may be reticent to test assumptions, to get out all of the issues, to probe for evidence and impact, to examine context, or query about constraints. They are unlikely to talk about time, people, or money, or elicit decision criteria. Critical information about the exact needs of the client may never surface.

> ❖ Communication will exhibit dilution, distortion, and generalization—it is unavoidable. How much is the only question.

One way to match and lead in this scenario is a "role reversal":

Match: I appreciate your offer. You've been very helpful so far.
Lead: May I share a concern? If you came to my company and my job was to get you the information from our key stakeholders, I could guarantee you at least two things:

1. I'd do my absolute best, and yet the communication would be filtered—it would be less than the original. And you would miss all the nuances.
2. I would not ask the same questions you would—you're the expert—so crucial information might never be communicated.

I'm imagining the same could happen here. I'd like to offer a suggestion. Do you know one of the key stakeholders well enough that you and I together could have about a thirty-minute conversation with him or her? At the end of our time, you can decide whether that time was well spent. If yes, you could extend it to another stakeholder. If not, all we risked was one thirty-minute conversation. Does that sound reasonable?

"Put Your Questions in Writing"

Let's say we put our questions in writing and give them to the client stakeholder. Hopefully, the client understands exactly what we are asking, since they won't be able to ask clarifying questions. The client writes down answers and gives them to us. We undoubtedly will have many follow-up questions that will either go unanswered or require another round of written exchange. The process is cumbersome, and the communication is usually much less rich than a conversation.

We might suggest to the gatekeeper that we write down our questions in advance and then the gatekeeper schedules a thirty-minute conversation between us and the stakeholder to talk them through. That way the questions will not be a mystery, the stakeholder won't have to take time to compose written responses, and both parties can ask and answer questions. It will be easier for the stakeholder and will likely be more informative for all concerned.

Playing the Percentages

The reasons gatekeepers give for not granting access are predictable and few. As consultants, we encounter them over and over. It is worth our time to create and practice responses that increase the probability we will get to talk with key stakeholders. If we never try, our probability of success will be low. If we always try, sometimes they will agree immediately. Sometimes they will offer a predictable response, and after talking it through with us, they will grant access. Sometimes, no matter how skilled we are, no matter how good our intent, they will say no. We can then decide to proceed anyway, or to gracefully offer to exit. If we give

> ❖ With good intent and good technique we will increase the percentage of times we meet personally with key client stakeholders.

good reasons for our exit, clients might even try to keep us in the process. Our willingness to "walk if we can't talk" may induce the client to be more flexible and creative.

Mahan had a consultant client who was working with a Fortune 100 company. She needed to see the board of directors to really have a grasp of what their needs were. As she tried to meet with people at such a high

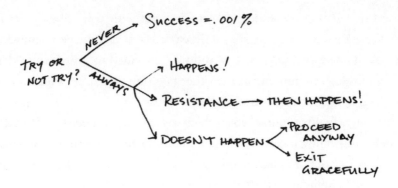

level, the main point of resistance was a gatekeeper determined to not give her access. So she said to the gatekeeper, "My company's only goal in this is to get you a solution that exactly meets your needs, and based on what you're telling me, the board of directors is the owner of those needs. To understand what [the directors] need, I will need to talk to them." The gatekeeper said, "That can't happen." So she made one move after another to get access, each one met with dogged resistance.

There were only three companies proposing, and her company was one of the top companies in this particular area. She said, "I respect your decision to not let me speak to the board. I don't agree with it, but I respect it. I hope you'll respect my decision not to propose. This is too important a project and has too high visibility to make guesses about what you need. I'll end up wasting everyone's time and potentially embarrassing my company. We're either going to end up looking ignorant or arrogant. I'm unwilling to commit my company's name or proposal when I don't understand what [the board] considers to be important."

The gatekeeper replied, "If you don't want to propose, then don't propose. That's your choice." She walked away, and had to tell her client manager what she had done. Luckily, her client manager had been through our course and backed her up; otherwise she might have had some serious problems, since this was a very big deal. She was at home that night (as she tells the story), saying to herself, "What have I done to my career? My family?" Then she received a call from her client manager, who said, "I just received a call from one of the directors of [the client's company]. They heard we weren't proposing and asked why. When I told him your reasons, he said that was crazy, and they want to meet with you." She eventually talked to everyone on the board of directors and had some great conversations. At its next meeting the board quickly decided to go with her company while scarcely looking at the other two bids. The one condition was that she manage the relationship.

Although that was admittedly a high-risk strategy, she was so committed to a solution that exactly met her client's needs that she was willing to walk away rather than guess. And when people understood her intent, not only did they invite her in, they gave her the business.

Leaving a "Back Door"

Before you match and lead, it may be helpful to leave a "back door," so if your counterpart refuses your logic, you still have a choice to continue.

The decision is ultimately the clients' call, and our job is to support their decision. The back door might therefore sound like "Bill, I know this is your responsibility, and my job is to support you in it. Whatever you decide is what we'll go with. Do you mind if I share some thoughts?"

Now you're ready to match and lead; if your contact doesn't concur, you haven't painted yourself into a corner. You can still say, "I appreciate your at least listening to me. As I said before, my job is to support you. If that's your decision, so be it."

> ❖ Don't paint yourself into a corner. This is something we want to fight for, not fight about.

If we get blocked in gaining access, we have some choices:

1. Chunk it down.
2. Go around.
3. Decide not to play.
4. Play anyway.

Chunk It Down

In the decision grid, there are often several steps, with different people in each step. We don't necessarily need an agreement to see all the people in all the steps before we can move forward even one step. At a minimum we need agreement to see the people in the step we are about to enter—before those people make their decision. For instance, if the first decision was to winnow down from six companies to three, we want to talk to the people making that decision. If the three get "passed on" to the selection committee," we want to talk with the selection committee members individually before they decide to "bump it up to the CEO." If the CEO is a decision maker, we want to talk to him or her before any decision is made.

Within a step, we can get permission to see one person at a time. We can ask our counterpart if there is one stakeholder with whom he or she feels comfortable and safe. Ask if the three of us can meet together. Only if our counterpart feels the conversation adds value will it be extended to another stakeholder. Our counterpart maintains control.

Go Around

It is clearly a high-risk tactic to go around your counterpart when he or she doesn't want you to. However, *you* don't have to do it. You can have someone "higher" than yourself in your organization talk to the person "higher" than your counterpart in the client organization. If the person higher than you is using the same lines of inquiry (issues and criteria), you will get the needed information.

Gaining access to key stakeholders is critical, yet it is something you want to fight for, not fight about. If you try to resolve the gatekeeper's objections a couple of different ways and are unsuccessful, you may want to exit through your "back door" and strategize with your colleagues. You may find someone other than you from your company who can gain access to the client stakeholder. You may then want to contact the gatekeeper and give him a heads-up with something like "Mike, I just got word that our CFO, Mary Johnson, is paying a courtesy call on your CFO, Mark Thomas. On an initiative of this magnitude she would consider it rude and bad business not to check in. I know you were against my meeting with Mark and I wanted to let you know I won't be in that meeting."

There is a risk in going around someone who doesn't want us to. There is a risk in not talking with key decision makers. We have to assess which risk is greater and how to best reduce the risk we choose to accept.

Decide Not to Play

When people are unwilling or unable to give us good information or access to people we need to see, we may decide that this is a fatal flaw in producing a viable solution. Whether innocently or due to ulterior motives, they render our involvement vulnerable—both in our ability to be selected and in our ability to produce a workable solution. We may feel that our time could be more productively spent with companies and people who want to interact more effectively. This could be a reason to "gracefully offer to exit."

Play Anyway

If we left a "back door," we still have the option of proceeding to the Exact Solution step, even though it isn't likely to be exact. Sometimes we figure that we have as good a chance of guessing as anyone else, and choose to roll the dice. As we will discuss in the Winning section, we should advocate for plenty of time to present our solution. We can use part of the presentation time to facilitate an Opportunity dialogue with the client stakeholders. We might start off by saying, "Our goal is to provide you with a solution that exactly meets your needs. Toward that end there are some things we know and some things we don't know. Your company has given us some good background information—sufficient to come here today with a good hypothesis of what will work. However, we haven't had a chance to speak with you personally and wouldn't feel comfortable making a final recommendation without more fully understanding your perspective on what needs to happen. Before we present our solution, would you mind if we ask you a few questions?"

Combining inquiry and advocacy in one meeting is not ideal, but it is definitely better than no inquiry at all.

What about the Time?

We could end up talking with a lot of people. That takes time. That time, used skillfully, is the single biggest differentiator in "making the sale." Whoever gains and uses that time the best wins—most of the time. We still must have a valid solution and present it well; that is the second biggest differentiator, not the first.

To gain the time you need, take time away from pursuing opportunities where you are not allowed to talk with people. Take time away from working on lengthy proposals with low probability of success. Take time away from sales activities that do not make sense.

> ❖ Engaging in rich dialogue with decision makers and influencers is the highest priority use of your time.
>
> Steal time away from low value-added activities (and clients) and invest it in developing mutual understanding with key stakeholders.

UNDERSTANDING DECISION CRITERIA

DECISION PROCESS EXAMPLE				
Steps	**Decision**	**When**	**Who**	**Criteria/Beliefs**
Talk to 6–8 Companies	Which 6–8?	May 15–June 1	Me	
Narrow to 3	Which 3? Defend choices	June 8	Me, End User, 1 Unit Head	How will each decision maker decide?
Pass on to Selection Committee	Recommend top choice and defend	June 15	CFO, CIO, SVP, 4 Unit Heads	
Refer to CEO	Confirm or push back	June 22–26	CEO	

Let's say we are granted access to the people we want to see. Now what? As much as possible, in the time available, we want to accomplish the following:

1. Understand the Opportunity from each person's perspective. What are the key issues, evidence, impact, context, and constraints? We may start with something like "Thank you very much for taking the time to meet with us. On an initiative of this nature, it is

critical we get your input and insight. *From your perspective as _____, what are the important issues this project must resolve?"*

> ❖ When people feel you have a good understanding of their criteria, they have more faith in you and your solution.

2. Understand stakeholders' criteria for deciding between alternatives.
3. Understand what they would like to see, hear, and experience in our presentation that would allow them to make a good decision.
4. Test out yellow lights.
5. Gain permission for another call, should it be helpful.

We've taken considerable time exploring how to structure the Opportunity conversation. Let's take a look at exploring criteria for deciding between alternatives. There are always alternatives. In addition to working with us, clients can decide to:

1. Do nothing.
2. Do it themselves.
3. Do it with someone other than us.

Consultants often say that two of their biggest competitors are "doing nothing" or "doing it themselves." If these are options, talk about them. Ask:

- "Is doing nothing an option?"
- "Are there competing uses of funds that might take precedence over this project?"
- "I get the sense that one viable option would be to do this yourselves. Have you given that any thought?"

If they answer yes to any of these questions, we then want to know "What would drive your decision *one way or the other?"* What specific criteria will they use to decide between doing nothing or doing something?

How will they decide whether to do it themselves or to do it with outside help?

External Competition

Understanding the competition can be an advantage and a disadvantage. It works against us if we focus more on the competition than on the client. It works for us when it gives us insight into how clients are thinking about their choices, and when it helps us differentiate our solution from the competition.

We will know whether or not there is external competition when eliciting the "steps" of the decision process; it will be clear during this process whether or not the client will be talking to other companies. It is simple to ask, "You mentioned you would be getting bids from other companies. Out of curiosity, who are you talking to?" With any reasonable rapport, they will tell us. Some clients *want* consultants to know who the competition is; they find it helpful if we can differentiate what we do versus what others do. Other clients feel it is somehow better to keep us in the dark. If they are reticent in sharing the names of the competitors, it can still be helpful to know the number and types of competitors.

Knowing the number of competitors can give us insight into how the client is thinking about alternatives. The smaller the number of competitors, the more likely the client has done due diligence and is ready to select; greater numbers suggest that a client is still in the information-gathering process. The type of competitor we are facing can be revealing. For instance, assume we are bidding on a process improvement initiative, and our competition includes two nontraditional providers—one firm known much more for strategy than process improvement and another firm known for process improvement in another industry. There are probably some good reasons for inviting the nontraditional players; it would be good to understand those reasons.

Even more important than knowing the names of our competitors, is understanding the clients' criteria for deciding among them.

> ❖ On what basis will the client choose between alternatives? What is the difference that will make the most difference?

Given that they have good companies to choose from, and that all those companies are going to claim, "We have really good people, we've done good things for others like you, we'll do good things for you," how is the client going to figure out which one is really the best? What are the differences that make a difference? What will the client need to see, hear, or experience before confidently making a decision.

Few clients keep a comprehensive list of criteria in their desk drawer, just waiting for the moment a consultant asks for it. They may not have thought out their reasons at all, nor tried to articulate them. They may use words that reflect a high level of abstraction, such as "creative," "leading edge," "value-added," "experienced," "dedicated," etc. With good inquiry skills we can add value in helping to articulate client beliefs and potentially help shape good criteria.

The Incumbent

If the client has been working with an incumbent, what is the motivation to change? Is this just a market check or price check, or is this a real opportunity? Usually, there is a transition cost associated with change. You can't be equal to the incumbent; you have to be demonstrably better.

> ❖ If there is an incumbent, why change?

What would be so compelling a difference that a client would actually kick out an incumbent? Let's make sure we find out.

Who Stands to Win/Lose?

The introduction of a solution purchased from an outside company may cause some people in the buying organization to feel they have won or lost. People who perceive themselves as benefiting could potentially champion our cause. People who perceive they are

> ❖ Does someone have a vested interest in this *not* happening?

losing may try to sabotage the deal. We will never know unless we ask.

We could say something like:

- "Clearly, the solution will help the organization. Yet, in thinking about all the people affected, is there anyone who stands to lose?"
- "Who might be perceived to win or lose, if this solution is adopted?"
- "This project seems to make a lot of sense for the organization as a whole. Is there anyone who would have a vested interest in the project *not* happening?"

If we find out there are people who perceive themselves at a disadvantage, we have two common choices: co-opt or counteract. We can talk to them and find out if there is a way to understand and meet their needs (co-opt). Or, if they are unwilling to honestly explore, we can ask our sponsors for ways to mitigate their impact (counteract).

Personal Stake

People tend to act in their own best interest. Organizations try to align individual interests with organizational priorities. Sometimes they are aligned and sometimes not. Fortunately, and increasingly, an individual cannot win unless he or she does something that makes the organization win; there is too much pressure to succeed in the competitive global market. Nonetheless, there are also conflicting rewards and goals within an organization. With sufficient time and rapport, understanding the personal and professional motivation of key stakeholders can be tremendously important. If we can understand how individuals stand to win or lose, we have a chance to align what's in their best interest with what's in the organization's best interest. We may even have the opportunity to have our solution resolve conflicting objectives, thus providing additional value.

We could ask:

- "On a scale of one to ten, how important is it to you *personally* that this project be successful?"
- "How would you personally win or lose if this initiative is adopted?"

Assuming everything has gone well, we are about to make a presentation to the client. We can either guess what should be in that presentation, or ask. Let's ask. What would clients have to intellectually and emotionally believe to be true before they could confidently make a final decision—one way or the other? What would they like to see, hear, or experience in the presentation that would be helpful in deciding? What have they found particularly irritating and counterproductive in other presentations?

In Conclusion

In a complex opportunity, we need to discuss Opportunity, Resources, and Decisions with many people. They will have different perspectives on *Opportunity* (issues, evidence, impact, context, and constraints). They may have differing opinions and knowledge about *Resources* (time, people, and money). They may have a different understanding of the *Decision Process* (the decisions, and who gets involved). They may have differing criteria for the decision. Let's find out. The better we understand the situation, the more likely we are to produce a solution that makes sense, is implemented, and succeeds.

The Decision Process

Steps	Decision	When	Who	Criteria/ Beliefs
What are all of the steps?	What decision gets made in each step?	When will they decide?	Who is involved in each step	How will each decision maker decide?

Competition:	How will they decide between alternative solutions?
Gain/Loss:	Who in the organization stands to win or lose if this solution is adopted?
Personal Stake:	How does the person we are talking with win or lose?

CHAPTER SIX

WINNING: THE ART

OF ENABLING DECISIONS

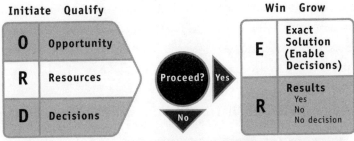

To advocate well is fun. At times it is exhilarating. The more skilled we become, the greater it feels. We learn to communicate the essence of our message from the core of our being. We clear our minds of all distractions, become highly aware and alert, completely present and in the moment. We sharpen our intellect and reason cogently and compellingly. We become grounded, centered, and more secure. We learn to be comfortable with strong emotions and sensitive to subtle ones. In groups, we are able to connect with each individual and deftly orchestrate interactions and outcomes that all can embrace.

This section is dedicated to the smile on our faces, the exuberance in our beings that comes from walking out of a meeting knowing everything came together like magic. All of our conversations and preparation were more than justified.

In Qualifying, we developed as much mutual understanding with the client as reasonably possible. We understand what is important for clients to achieve, what resources they have available, and how they make decisions. If we have done a good job of inquiry, clients also have more insight and feel we understand them and their business. The foundation of good relationships is in place.

By the time we enter the Winning phase, we *want* to win this business, and feel we can. Now is our opportunity to effectively advocate our solution and gain a favorable decision.

The phrase "enabling decisions" connotes that the decisions themselves are enabling; they enable clients to get what they want in a way they feel good about. The phrase also refers to a consultant's ability to be a catalyst, a facilitator of the decision; we enable decisions by presenting them in an intellectually and emotionally compelling manner.

There are two major keys to winning deals more consistently. First, don't present until you are ready to present. Second, when you do present, present to enable a decision.

DON'T PRESENT UNTIL YOU ARE READY TO PRESENT

Many consultants present to open rather than to close. They are so enthusiastic about their solution that they present it at the very first opportunity. Unfortunately, more often than not they are guessing about what will be convincing to the client and they are often presenting to people who are not authorized to say yes. Are we surprised their win rate is low? (And when win rates are low, management ironically often pushes to do *more* proposals rather than improve quality.) Quantity over quality starts to prevail, creating a losing situation for all parties.

When we present our solution, the objective is to have everything and everyone necessary for a decision together in the same place at the same time. *We present, they decide.* Done. If we present and they *cannot* decide, we presented prematurely.

> ❖ Have everyone and everything necessary for a decision in the same place at the same time. We present, they decide.

You are ready when:

1. You have completed sufficient ORD (Opportunity, Resources, Decisions) discussions with the people who influence and make the decision. You are presenting to people whose criteria for judging you are known to you.

> ❖ Only present to people whose criteria for judging you are known to you.

2. You are presenting *in person* to:
   a. The right people
   b. For the right amount of time.

We have talked in depth in the Qualifying sections about gaining access to and having good ORD dialogue with key stakeholders. Let's examine the remaining elements of readiness.

> ❖ Present in person, to the right people, for the right amount of time.

Present in Person

Proposals don't sell, people do. Why go through all the effort to talk extensively to several people and then relegate our findings to pieces of paper? Proposals are horrible selling vehicles. They can be appropriate to confirm what has already been agreed to, to prepare decision makers in advance, and to leave behind as a reference document of the details and facts. However, if we are counting on a written document to do our selling for us, we are in trouble.

> ❖ Sign in Las Vegas: You must be present to win.

The bad news about formal proposals is that most (not all) are poorly composed, poorly written, include a lot of unnecessary information, are hard to comprehend, and are usually much too long. The good news? Nobody reads them anyway. One study showed that decision makers spend about five minutes per proposal. What will they look at in five minutes? The price and some overview of what you want to say.

What do we have in person that we lack in writing?

Vocal cues: We can hear the tone, emphasis, inflection, and pace of language. (Can you remember a time when you sent an e-mail or a letter that you thought was very funny—it sounded funny when you said it to yourself—but was dead on arrival?)

Visual cues: We get powerful nonverbal feedback.

Interaction: There is give and take; we can respond to questions, address concerns, and react.

Flexibility: If something is not working, we can change; we can react to new developments, challenges, and directions.

Rapport: People feel who we are as human beings, and vice versa.

Mutual understanding: It's hard to come to a true meeting of the minds in a written document.

Closure: We have the opportunity to conclude with a decision, or to know what it would take to get one.

> ❖ Proposals don't sell—people do.

Why would we—or the client—ever give up these benefits? It usually happens like this: The client says, "Send me a proposal," and we say, "Okay." It's what we are used to doing. But we can do better.

General Rule: Do not present in writing what you could present in person.

We desire a meeting where we can present our solution as an interactive oral presentation that allows give and take: "If we did this, would it be a solution that meets your needs? If not, where does it have to change?"

A general thought process for suggesting an in-person meeting is:

1. I think we have a good understanding of what you would like to accomplish, what resources are available, and how you'd like to make this decision.
2. What I would like to do now is:
   - Meet with my team.
   - Develop our best thinking on a solution that exactly meets your needs.
   - Have my team meet with your team.
   - Have you challenge our best thinking with your best thinking.
3. I'm confident of two things:

a. You will be excited about some of the things we come up with.

b. Something will be missing, not quite right, or could be improved with changes. Meeting together will allow us to understand what makes sense and what doesn't.

4. After that meeting, we'll write up our findings in a formal document, give it to you, and you can make whatever decision is in the best interest of your company. Does that sound reasonable?

The "formal document" we write should be a confirmation letter or an agreement, not a proposal. The buying discussion will happen in the face-to-face meeting.

The message we want to convey is: WE *ARE* THE PROPOSAL! When the client asks, "When can you send me a proposal?" we can say, "Well, we *are* the proposal. When would you like to meet with us?"

> ❖ We are the proposal. When would you like to meet?

Yes or No?

Sometimes presenting in person is a normal part of the buying process and therefore is not an issue; written proposals are followed by "orals" or a product demonstration. In situations where we are the only company involved, gaining agreement for oral presentations should not be a problem, as long as we make a good case for it. In competitive situations, some clients will agree to in-person presentations; others will respond with some predictable push-backs:

- "We don't have the time."
- "It wouldn't be fair."
- "If we let you do it, we would have to let everyone do it."
- "Why can't you just send the proposal?"

Remember our intent? We want a solution that exactly meets their needs. Remember what we have in person that we do not have in writing? Neither the client, nor we, should compromise at this critical juncture. Clients have sometimes spent years getting to the point where something needs to change. They are about to make a decision the consequences of which they will live with for a long time. Proposals do not do the work. Proposals do not help clients succeed. People do. It is in clients' best interest to allow sufficient opportunity for solution providers to fully explain their ideas, to ask them good questions, to test assumptions, and to experience what the people are like to work with.

Despite our best efforts, the client may insist on a written proposal. Perhaps it is a screening device to reduce many companies to a few. Perhaps it is "policy," and it is not open to examination. If that is the case, then:

1. Try to gain agreement for an in-person preproposal meeting, a trial run, a draft session with one or more key stakeholders—to test out your thinking. It doesn't make sense or serve anyone to commit to writing that which doesn't make sense to the client.
2. Failing that, try for a telephone review of the main elements with one or more key stakeholders—for the same reasons as above.
3. Failing that, gain agreement to present—not just deliver—your formal written proposal in person.

Only if all else fails will we send a formal written proposal in the mail, with no human interaction. This is a major yellow light. Optimal decisions happen person-to-person, not computer-to-computer.

Present to the Right People

Our objective is to enable a decision. We cannot do that if the people in the room cannot decide. That is obvious. Yet many times consultants present to people who will then take their impressions from that presentation to someone else, who will then make the decision. It is unlikely that the people presenting on our behalf will do as good a job as we will. They will not answer questions with the same ability, authority, or credibility. We would be shocked if they did as good a job of resolving doubts, stalls, concerns, or objections, or of pushing against faulty or inaccurate thinking—particularly if they are working with organizational superiors. So why would consultants agree to have someone other than themselves present the solution? Often because clients say that is how they are going to do it, and consultants merely comply.

Consultants who have done a good job in qualifying have leverage. Clients should now feel the consultant understands them and their business, and are curious to see what solution we come up with. If we have not been premature in offering a solution or a written proposal, the client's curiosity should be piqued rather than sated. Also, if we have talked with the key stakeholders, we have had the opportunity to gain their agreement to attend the presentation.

Consultants should use their leverage to present only when those people necessary for the decision are present. If all the people necessary for the decision are not present in one meeting, gain prior agreement to meet with them in subsequent meetings.

One of Mahan's clients flew four of their top executives from Chicago to London to meet with the CEO of a prospective client. Upon their arrival, the CEO called to apologize. He had to fly out immediately to attend to an emergency with his company's best customer. He genuinely wanted to meet, but the situation with the customer was critical. He asked the four executives to meet with his leadership team who would fill him in later. The four executives knew that the CEO's attendance was crucial. No matter how well they interacted with the leadership team, it would be impossible to get a decision. They knew that the leadership team, no matter how well-intended, could not be as persuasive with the CEO as they could.

They told the CEO that they understood and respected his priority; they would have made the same decision. They said that meeting with him and the leadership team *together* was a priority as well. They got on a plane, flew back to Chicago, and rescheduled the meeting. When they returned to London two weeks later, they were treated royally, had everyone's full attention, and landed a very substantial new account.

Present for the Right Amount of Time

What is the amount of time clients allot for a typical sales presentation? Often it is one hour, with forty-five minutes for presentation and fifteen minutes for questions and answers. Of course, if we are talking about typical meetings, they do not start on time; the topics are often complex; presenters nearly always run over their allotted time; questions and answers are sacrificed. No decision gets made.

> ❖ Time is money. Make sure you get enough of it.

It is very difficult to arrive at a decision when there is insufficient time to fully explore thinking and to ask and answer questions. Such meetings tend to end with, "Thank you very much for coming," rather than with a well-thought-out decision.

You benefit everyone when you make a compelling case for presenting solutions only with sufficient time to arrive at good decisions. Clients should not constrain richness of dialogue at the riskiest phase of their buying process—the point at which they must choose their best course of action. If time is the real issue, spending sufficient time to make a good decision is the best use of time.

If you have not been allowed sufficient access and time to interview key stakeholders *before* presenting your solution, you are well advised to build *even more* time into the presentation. You can then allow ample time to arrive at mutual agreement on the Opportunity and Decision Criteria before discussing the solution.

THE MEETING PLAN—PRESENT TO ENABLE A DECISION

The purpose of a sales presentation is to enable a decision. It is not to inform or educate, though that may be helpful. It is not to entertain, though that may be enjoyable. The purpose is to enable a decision. We present, they decide.

> ❖ The purpose of a sales presentation is to enable a decision.

There are certainly multiple ways to enable a decision. The presentation format offered here has been successful in diverse applications throughout the world. It is a powerful choice to add to your repertoire. A visual representation of the format is shown in the accompanying graphic:

Let's Get Real or Let's Not Play

· Must find a "Better Way" of Selling

· All tied to needs

The Purpose of a Presentation Is to...
Enable a Decision!

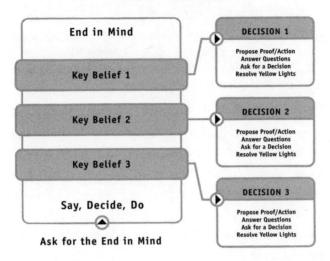

| End in Mind | | **DECISION 1** |
| Key Belief 1 | | Propose Proof/Action
Answer Questions
Ask for a Decision
Resolve Yellow Lights |

The elements of this presentation are represented in the following Meeting Plan. The authors and many of our clients use the same Meeting Plan for final presentations as we do for other client meetings. We use them for in-person meetings and telephone calls. Some companies use the name "Call Plan" rather than "Meeting Plan." You will encounter the Meeting Plan again in the Initiating section.

MEETING PLAN

End in Mind (EIM)	What do we want the client to say, do, decide at the end of the meeting? How will we gain agreement to the EIM before or at the beginning of the meeting?
Key Beliefs	What will the client likely need to believe, intellectually and emotionally, to comfortably decide on the EIM?
Proof/Action	What proof or proposed action will we provide to address the key beliefs?

Questions	What would we most like to know from the client? How will we ask? What questions is the client likely to ask? How will we respond?
Yellow Lights	What reasons might the client have for not deciding or deciding not in our favor (stalls, doubts, concerns, objections)? How will we address them?
Next Steps	What next steps, if any, should we be prepared to offer?
Agenda	What is a concise agenda that integrates all of the above? How can we best gain agreement to the agenda?

The elements in the Meeting Plan are purposefully few. Each is discussed in depth within this section.

End in Mind

Start with the End in Mind. If we agree that the purpose of a sales presentation is to enable a decision, then a critical determination is what, specifically, do we want the client to *say, do,* or *decide* at the end of our presentation? The authors refer to this ultimate decision as the End in Mind. If we can gain the clients' agreement to the End in Mind—at the beginning of the meeting (or before the meeting)—it is much more likely that we can return to it at the end of the meeting and gain a decision.

> ❖ Start with the End in Mind: what do we want the client to say, do, or decide at the end of our interaction?

Here are some common deficiencies that interfere with establishing a good End in Mind.

```
┌─────────────────────────────┐
│                             │
│   MEETING PLAN              │
│   ─────────────             │
│                             │
│   End in Mind               │
│   Key Beliefs               │
│   Proof/Action              │
│   Questions                 │
│   Yellow Lights             │
│   Next Steps                │
│   Agenda                    │
│                             │
└─────────────────────────────┘
```

1. *There is no clear End in Mind.*

Pull out ten or more presentations from your organization. How many of them, right in the beginning, make it completely clear what the client is being asked to say, do, or decide at the end of the presentation? Our prediction is very few. Most presentations have an agenda with some discussion of "our team," "our approach/methodology," "our product/service," "our tools/skills," "our experience," "our price/fees," and perhaps even "our understanding," etc. The agenda may end with "Questions?" and "Next Steps." The presentation is all about the consultant and not the client. What specifically is the client supposed to decide?

If the decision to be made is not clear to either the consultants or the clients, how likely is it that a decision will be made?

2. *The End in Mind for this presentation is unrealistic or inappropriate.*

If we are in initial meetings and we state our End in Mind as "Do you want to buy our product or service today?" it could be wildly inappropriate (yet more common than one would expect). A more appropriate End in Mind might be "Is there sufficient interest that we should keep talking, or is it thanks, but no thanks?" The End in Mind should reasonably move us forward, without overreaching.

If we are in a competitive situation, we would like to know if they are going to buy from us or one of the competitors; however, that would likely be an inappropriate End in Mind, particularly if we are not the last presenter. A more effective End in Mind for a competitive final presentation is some version of "Is this a solution that truly meets your needs?" or a more watered down approach, "Do you feel you have all the information you need to make a well-informed decision?"

3. *The End in Mind is poorly worded and engenders client resistance.*

Rather than providing a true choice for the client, some consultants state the End in Mind as the answer they want to hear. It might sound like "We feel confident you will say at the end of this meeting that you want to work with us." There are many people who, if they feel you are driving them to *your* conclusion rather than helping them reach their own conclusion, will move aggressively in the opposite direction of what you intended. These people resent being corralled.

Remember, "If you want good information on what it takes to get a *yes,* make *no* be okay." When most people feel they have the freedom to make a true choice, they are more willing to commit to making a decision.

Here are some examples:

"We assume you are counting on us, during this meeting, to give you sufficient information to decide that either our solution makes sense—"Let's do it"—or does not make sense, and you'll pass. Is that what you were expecting as well?"

"We've all been working together on the XYZ initiative for six months. In our last meeting the choice on the table was 'Should we do this initiative now or should we wait?' You decided not to wait. Today the question seems to be 'Should you do this with our company's help or would another option better serve you.' Is that what you were hoping to decide as well?"

"We appreciate the opportunity to be here today. We realize you have three very good solution providers to select from. We also understand the choice is critical, that this is a 'bet the company' initiative and it is absolutely imperative that you 'get it right.' That is the test we would like to offer today as we present our solution: 'Did we get it right? If not, what would have to change?' We realize that if someone else gets it 'more right'—if they have an even better solution—then you will pick them. Knowing that, would you be willing to give us candid feedback on whether or not you could say with confidence, that at least one solution got it right?"

The End in Mind should seem logical for where you are in the buying process. It should seem reasonable. It should feel like intelligent businesspeople would be concerned and feel their time was wasted if we *were not* going to reach that decision.

In initiating opportunities, the End in Mind is often, "Should we be talking?" In qualifying, it is often, "Should we keep talking?" In enabling decisions, it often takes the form "Should you do this with us?"

4. *There is failure to gain client agreement on the End in Mind either before the meeting or at the beginning of the meeting.*

The authors strongly recommend testing the meeting agenda with the client before the meeting. That agenda includes the End in Mind and the path for getting to the End in Mind decision. If the client agrees, it establishes the focus for the meeting.

If not accomplished before the meeting, gaining agreement to the End in Mind should come at the beginning of the meeting. This should sound obvious. Good presentations are not like good mystery novels, which you read eagerly to the end to find out what happened. Good presentations give the conclusion up-front and spend the rest of the time revealing how you got there.

Here is an example of ignoring the obvious: The authors, Mahan and Randy, were making a joint call on the CEO of a highly desirable prospective client. They had worked on a Meeting Plan and developed an End in Mind for the meeting. They got agreement on the End in Mind and agenda from their sponsor, a senior vice president, but not directly from the CEO. When the meeting started, the SVP gave a long, rambling, and unplanned introduction. Mahan, in an attempt to weave what he wanted to accomplish into the SVP's monologue, began asking the CEO questions from the questions prepared on the meeting plan. He then adroitly tried to cover some of the key beliefs as they appeared in the conversation. At no time was the End in Mind explicitly introduced. And lo and behold, after what was a very friendly and informative chat, no decision was reached other than to keep talking. Randy started the postmeeting debriefing with the question, "And the purpose of this meeting was . . . ?" Even though the meeting ended indecisively, everything eventually worked out—yet it took much longer than necessary. Pain is often the best teacher.

Key Beliefs

```
MEETING PLAN

End in Mind
Key Beliefs
Proof/Action
Questions
Yellow Lights
Next Steps
Agenda
```

Stepping Stones to the End in Mind

Once we know where we want to be at the end of the meeting, the next step is to decide how best to get there in the allotted amount of time. Apparently a great number of consultants believe that the "best way" to get to a decision is to overwhelm clients with massive amounts of information about their company and solution. They create presentations that are information-rich, yet unfortunately, decision-poor. Consultants seriously hinder, rather than facilitate, a decision when:

- They give the client far more information than what is necessary for the decision; they waste valuable time, potentially confuse the client, and risk introducing doubts, concerns, and objections that otherwise would never appear.
- The information comes in one big glut with questions and decisions held to the end; the information is not organized into bite-sized pieces that are easy to digest.
- It is not clear what questions in the clients' mind the information is intended to answer; there are no decisions made at the end of each agenda item.
- The information is about the consultant company and not the client.

- The information is not explicitly linked to client issues and decision criteria. The information is not linked to the End in Mind.

To enable a decision, the first guideline is "Start with the End in Mind"; the second guideline is "Give only the information necessary for the decision." In inquiry we say, "No guessing." In advocacy, we say, "Nothing Extra."

> ❖ Only give clients what they need in order to decide on the End in Mind. Nothing extra.

Rather than asking clients to make one big leap over a large pond of information, we give them several stepping stones placed a reasonable distance apart from one another, which makes traversing the pond easier, more enjoyable—and keeps the client from falling into the pond and drowning in information. We should have no fewer, and no more, stepping stones than are helpful to get from the beginning of the meeting to the End in Mind. The general rule of thumb is to have between three to seven steps.

Key beliefs are one type of stepping stone. Depending on the situation, other means of reaching the End in Mind may well serve us better. Nonetheless, thinking through key beliefs is almost always helpful.

Would you consider the following statements to be true or false?

- People make decisions based on beliefs (what they believe to be true or false, good or bad, valuable or not valuable, practical or impractical, understandable or confusing, etc.).
- Those beliefs are often not explicit (clients do not hand you a sheet of paper with their beliefs).
- Those beliefs are often not well-formed (they are not articulate, precise, or organized in a logical sequence).
- Those beliefs are not always commonly shared among key stakeholders.

If you answered true to any or all of the above, would you say the following is also true?

- We are more likely to enable the End in Mind if we can explicitly state and resolve the underlying beliefs that support that decision.

If you answered with a resounding "false," you might want to stop here. Otherwise, keep reading.

Two belief systems we can work with are:

> ❖ People make decisions based on beliefs. We are more likely to enable the End in Mind if we can explicitly state and resolve the underlying beliefs that support that decision.

The client's beliefs: What would clients have to intellectually and emotionally believe before they could confidently and comfortably make the End in Mind decision?

Our beliefs: What do we believe we must communicate in order for the client to decide on the End in Mind?

In general, the authors give preference to client beliefs and augment them only as necessary with our beliefs. Resolving clients' beliefs is more convincing to them and may be all they need to feel comfortable making a decision. Anything extra we introduce may confuse or complicate the decision.

Typical beliefs about a final presentation for a solution include:

- The solution will resolve the client's problems and produce the client's desired results.
- The solution can be implemented with the available resources.
- The solution meets the decision criteria of key stakeholders.
- The economics are compelling.
- This solution exceeds the alternatives.

Typical beliefs about the solution providers are:

- They are competent (they have the right expertise).
- They are credible (they will do what they say they will do).
- They are compatible (we will like working with them).

While these beliefs may be typical for solutions in general, the key beliefs and how they are worded are unique to each situation and presentation. When we meet with key stakeholders, we can elicit their beliefs with questions like: "Thinking forward to the presentation, what would you like to make sure we cover that will allow you to make a good decision, whether you choose us or someone else?" Or, "What would you like to see, hear, or experience in the presentation that would allow you to make a good decision, one way or the other?"

If the client agrees to the End in Mind and the key beliefs, we have a structure well-suited to enable a decision.

Proof/Action

```
MEETING PLAN

End in Mind
Key Beliefs
Proof/Action
Questions
Yellow Lights
Next Steps
Agenda
```

For each key belief we provide convincing proof or propose action to address that belief. Since we understand their issues in order of priority, we demonstrate to clients how our product or service gives them the ability to resolve them. Since we understand their decision criteria, we propose how we will meet them. Because we understand what resources are available, we confirm they will be used productively.

We have been patient about not presenting our solution prematurely. We now present it as compellingly as we can. Our goal is to give them precisely what they need to know to satisfy each belief—nothing less and nothing extra. The only way we will know if we have succeeded is to ask the client. We want to check off each key belief as we go, rather than wait until the end. If all of the key beliefs are satisfied, deciding on the End in Mind should be easy.

Asking for a Decision

Our goal in asking for a decision is to find out what the client believes to be true in reaction to what we have proposed. If we do not ask for a decision, we may be racing through yellow lights or losing the ability to build momentum when lights are green. However, asking for the decision *inappropriately* may cause clients to feel we are being manipulative or coercive. They may judge against us, even if they like our solution. We want the way we ask for a decision to be nonthreatening to the client while still accurately eliciting their thoughts and feelings.

Here are some possible ways to ask for a decision:

Free-form question: In situations where there are only one or two people, we might ask, "Before we proceed, how comfortable are you that this issue has been addressed to your satisfaction?" Or, "I know this is your top issue and I don't want to proceed until you are comfortable that it's been well addressed. What's your sense?" Or, "We are at the point where we should check this one off or know that we can't. What would you like to do?"

Scale of One to Ten: "Before we proceed, let me check in and see how we're doing. On a scale of one to ten, with ten being that we have addressed this issue to your satisfaction and one being that we've completely missed the boat, where are you?" (Some people will not give anything a ten, no matter how it is defined. A nine or even eight is as close as you will get, and that may be all you need.)

Red, Yellow, Green: The authors have given clients actual red, yellow, or green cards, to be used both with a sense of fun and a sense of purpose. At key decision points the clients are asked to hold up one of the three. The same can be done without cards by just asking how many of those present are green, yellow, or red.

"Fist to Five": If clients hold up five fingers it is green light; a fist is a red light. Four fingers could be okay or something to explore. Three or two fingers is a yellow light. One finger extended might be a clear signal it is time to leave.

Electronic voting: For large groups, or groups where it is helpful to keep votes anonymous, use of electronic voting pads that show the collective votes on a screen can be helpful. There can be several types of votes (yes/no; true/false; one to ten; multiple choice; etc.) and the voting itself can be fun as well as informative.

Put some thought into how you will ask for a decision on each key belief and on the final End in Mind. While asking in a natural and non-pressured way, you want to ensure the decision is firm and unequivocal.

Questions

MEETING PLAN

End in Mind
Key Beliefs
Proof/Action
Questions
Yellow Lights
Next Steps
Agenda

There are two types of questions to plan for: questions we want answered by the client and questions the client will likely have for us.

Questions for the client: Even with good inquiry, and sometimes as a result of good inquiry, we are likely to have burning questions that have not been answered. There may be missing pieces of analysis; perhaps we are unclear on the criteria for deciding; there may be suspicions about unresolved constraints. Think through what you really want to know. Emphasize priority over completeness: if you could only get answers to three questions, what would they be? Then prepare how and when you will get answers to those questions during the presentation.

Questions for the consultants: Client questions are often predictable. The more difficult the question, the more helpful it is to prepare our answers in advance.

Answering the Real Question

During the presentation, when the client asks a question, it often masks the real question. Here is an example:

A good friend of Mahan's—now a great sales trainer—used to be a salesperson for a computer company Mahan founded. Mahan and his friend made many joint calls, learned and grew tremendously together. His friend had worked on a significant sale for about six months, and was making his final presentation to the CEO and key decision makers. At the end of his presentation, about which everyone seemed enthusiastic, the CEO asked him, "I like what you've shown us. How big is your company?" His friend's fear at this point was that this sizable company would think Mahan's company was too small to execute and support such a large installation. He proceeded to conjure up every statement he could to make them seem big. The CEO listened patiently, then said, "Gosh, sounds like you're pretty big. That's too bad. We just worked with a large computer company and they ignored us. We won't make the same mistake again. We are committed to working with a small company who will give us the best service possible. But thank you for coming out to visit us."

The real question in this situation was not "How big is your company?" It was "Will you give us good service?" If Mahan's friend had known service was the real question, he could have skillfully addressed it. Without knowing the real question, he addressed his own fear. With a small investment of time, he could well have uncovered the real concern.

Some possible responses might have been: "We are a $__million company. I sense you're asking for a reason. Is the size of the company important to your decision?" Or, "I'd be glad to talk about the size of our company and I sense you're asking for a reason. Could you share the reason?"

Mahan's friend now says, "The question they ask you is *never* the real question!" Perhaps he is just stressing the point. He was able to salvage this opportunity, yet he had to dig himself out of an unnecessary hole to do so.

People ask a question for a reason. Sometimes the reason seems obvious. Many times the reason is obscure. Without knowing the reason, we risk answering the wrong question. In doing so, we waste valuable time and bore the client. Even worse, we introduce questions and doubts in the client's mind that did not previously exist.

> ❖ People ask questions for a reason. Don't guess about the reason or you may not answer the real question; you may answer the wrong question or introduce even more questions or yellow lights in the client's mind.

People use questions in order to think. Thinking is an internal dialogue of asking and answering questions. You might wonder "Is that true? Do I do that? Does everyone do that? Do we do it all the time? Can we think without asking questions?" People often ask questions in order to stimulate their own thinking. If we encourage them to keep going, they frequently continue to explore their train of thought. If we interfere with a lengthy response, we may derail their train of thought completely.

Having the patience to find the real question is particularly important in group situations. An individual in the group may ask a question to jump-start his own or the group's thinking. How the question is asked may be intended to impress or influence other group members. The question may be asked in a way that is designed to support a point of view. Clients may ask provocative questions to see how the consultant responds or to purposefully show the consultant in a bad light. In all these cases, we are well served to stay centered, resist immediate responses, and encourage the individual to say more.

Unfortunately, few consultants have the discipline to "stay out of the way." It has been engrained in us since childhood, that when a question is asked, we answer it. The pattern becomes even more entrenched when we become consultants and feel we are experts who know (or should know) all the answers. The issue here is not about knowing the answer; it is about knowing the real question.

A useful tool in our repertoire is "redirection." Redirection is answering a question with a question, which can be a powerful communication vehicle or a potentially irritating device. If we use the following technique with good intent, most of the time clients will either not notice, or not care, that we redirected their question.

Remember the *intent* of redirection is to:

- Understand and answer the real question.
- Avoid answering the wrong question.
- Allow clients to keep talking if that is what they really want to do.

The formula for redirection is:

Listening + Softening + Redirection Question = Successful Redirection

Listening: If we listen carefully to how the client words the question, it can guide us in how to phrase our redirection question.

> CLIENT: How will you make sure our communication to employees is highly professional?
> CONSULTANT: Several things come to mind. First, just so I don't guess, highly professional to you would mean . . . ?

Softening: The brain works on pattern recognition. When the client asks a question, the expected pattern is a response. If we answer immediately with a question, that breaks the pattern and can be jarring. ("How long will this take?" "How long do you think it should take?") If instead, we answer with a statement, and then ask our question, it better fits the expected pattern. We do not seem rude, confrontational, or annoying.

Examples of softening statements might be:

- "I appreciate your asking . . ."
- "Hmmm, good question . . ."
- "Thanks for bringing that up . . ."
- "Hmmm. I hadn't thought of that . . ."
- "The same question just occurred to me . . ."
- "Several things come to mind . . ."
- "I definitely have some opinions on that. Before I bias you . . ."

> CLIENT: Can you tell me about your methodology?
> CONSULTANT: I'd be happy to. I could probably talk enthusiastically

for a couple of hours. Did you want me to address something in particular?

A good softening statement can be a short answer to the question:

- "Yes, we do."
- "No, we don't."
- "The short answer is . . ."

Redirection Question: The key is to follow the answer with a redirection question. For example:

> CLIENT: How long does it take to implement a project like this?
> CONSULTANT: Typically three to six months. Do you have some time pressures or targets we should be aware of?

Here is an important caveat: If the client asks the same question twice, that is likely their real question. Answer it the best you can.

> CLIENT: How will we know you are the best company to work with?
> CONSULTANT: Well, let's talk about that. What would be your criteria for "best"?
> CLIENT: I want to know what *you* think makes you the best company.
> CONSULTANT: I think what we do particularly well is . . .

The key is awareness and choice. Be acutely aware that when a question is asked, you have an equal choice to either answer or to redirect. Develop the skill of redirection (listen, soften, redirect) so that you can execute the choice with expertise (the client usually won't notice or care). We might redirect only a few times during a conversation, but the impact can be huge; we can improve clients' thinking, address their real issues, and prevent creating unnecessary difficulties for ourselves.

Yellow Lights

```
┌─────────────────────────────┐
│                             │
│   MEETING PLAN              │
│   ───────────              │
│                             │
│   End in Mind               │
│   Key Beliefs               │
│   Proof/Action              │
│   Questions                 │
│   Yellow Lights             │
│   Next Steps                │
│   Agenda                    │
│                             │
└─────────────────────────────┘
```

Our goal is to enable a decision. A yellow light is a signal that the client will not decide at all or will not decide in our favor. If there were yellow lights that appeared in the qualifying process, we already turned them to green or red. Nonetheless, before a client decides and commits, any unresolved yellow lights are likely to appear either when we are presenting and have influence, or after we have left and have no influence. The success or failure of huge investments of time, energy, and money can hinge on our skill in uncovering and resolving critical yellow lights while present with the client.

There are two prevalent characteristics in consultants who are particularly adept at turning yellow lights to green: they check their ego at the door, and they are willing to be wrong.

1. The consultant is able to check his or her ego at the door.

We all have an ego (so it seems), and our ego is focused on getting *our* needs met—that's what egos do. Often our response to client objections or challenges is to defend or attack, which can evoke a counterdefense from the client. Sometimes we seek approval or acceptance and tend to agree to things we should not. At other times we want to show how smart or skilled we are and may impress ourselves more than the client. In contrast, top consultants are not distracted by their own needs and insecurities. They have a knack for staying centered, calm, objective, and clearheaded, even under pressure. In fact, the more the pressure, the deeper their calm.

Gerry Spence (author of *How to Win an Argument Every Time*) tells the following story: "The Spanish matadors had a phrase for dealing with the onslaught of the beast—'Ver llegar.' " Hemingway explained the meaning of the phrase in *Death in the Afternoon*: 'the ability to watch the bull come as he charges with no thought, except to calmly see what he is doing and make the moves necessary to the maneuver you have in mind. To calmly watch the bull come is the most necessary and primarily difficult thing in bullfighting.' So it is when one faces a charging *Other*, a judge, an opponent, a witness, a boss. By sheer concentration one watches the charge calmly with one's ears. If we choose, we can observe the *Other's* aggression come spewing out, and, *at our will*, we can also permit the noise to bounce off the walls like rattling cans."

Checking our ego is a skill we can learn and improve. It requires practice. When it becomes second nature we can choose clarity over commotion in response to client challenges.

2. The consultant is willing to be wrong.

It is not the goal to turn every yellow light to green. The goal is to win the business only when there is a good fit between what the client needs and what we do well. The authors have clients who have suffered hundreds of millions of dollars in operational losses, and billions of dollars in reduced market value, due to deals they "won" which they later wished they had "lost." If there is a fatal flaw in the solution, *we* want to discover it as much as the client does. If the client buys our solution and it is an abysmal failure, we lose as well. Consultants who are certain they are "right" tend to not fully listen to what clients are saying; they fail to examine assumptions and presuppositions; they push harder on what makes sense to them, rather than identifying and removing the causes of client resistance. In contrast, consultants who are willing to be wrong (even those of us who never have been) tend to gain credibility, deeper understanding, insight, and rapport. They more often turn yellow lights to green.

Never Do Something for Nothing

It is common for consultants to reach the end of a presentation, ask for the End in Mind, and receive instead a client request that effectively says "Please go away and do something." Rather than making a decision, the client wants us to get more information, wants to talk to references, requests us to write up a summary of what was discussed, needs us to present to some previously undisclosed stakeholder, and so on. Perhaps the request indicates a last missing piece of the decision puzzle and when provided makes the decision easy and favorable. Perhaps the client would rather assign a task than make a decision. It sometimes seems that clients have learned that "If you want to get rid of consultants, give them something to do."

> ❖ "When we make proposals to people, and their response is "We need to study it more," or "We need to refer it to a task force," or "We need to set up a committee," or "We need to check with other people to see how they feel about it," the other people may, in essence, be saying that our idea is not one that they can support, but they cannot tell us that they cannot support it." —*Chris Arygris,* Overcoming Organizational Defenses

In response to such decision-avoidant requests, the authors suggest the "Never Do Something for Nothing Redirection." It has two parts:

1. Define success: Find out what is really needed and how it is important.
2. Hypothetically walk into the future, give them success, and ask: "Then what happens?"

For instance, you ask for the End in Mind and the client asks to see more detail on some of your financial calculations; you do not have those with you. A possible two-part response might be:

STEP ONE: "I'd be glad to get those for you. Just to make sure I make good use of your time, what specifically would you like to see that would help you make a good decision, one way or the other?"

(Client responds.)

STEP TWO: "Great. Just so I understand how you would like to proceed, let's say we are a week in the future, you get this information in the way that you requested, and it makes good sense; then what happens?

If the client says, "Then we go with you," or at least, "Then we will decide" (and if you know the information is available and positive), get the information and the decision. If they say anything other than that they would make a decision, it is fair to push back: "I'm confused. It seems that even if I were to get you what you want, just the way you want it, it would not help you say yes *or* no. What's missing?"

If we are asked to "go away and do something," we need to understand what is wanted and what will happen if they get it. Never do something for nothing.

Acknowledge, Understand, Resolve

Here is a highly effective pattern for resolving nonprice yellow lights.

ACKNOWLEDGE: Demonstrate vocally and visually that you are slowing down for the yellow light.

UNDERSTAND: Ask questions to understand the true nature of the client's resistance and what the resolution would be.

RESOLVE: Work to a mutual resolution of the genuine issues at hand.

ACKNOWLEDGE

To acknowledge, we exhibit empathy and appreciation, *although not necessarily agreement*, with the client's reason for not moving forward. Acknowledging benefits from our ability to check our ego at the door and our willingness to be wrong. Examples of acknowledging include:

- "Well, let's talk about that."
- "I definitely hear the concern."
- "I appreciate your honesty."
- "Tough question. Good question, just tough to answer. Let's talk it through."
- "I definitely want to share some thoughts on that."
- "If we can't find some good answers to that, I wouldn't want either of us to proceed."

UNDERSTAND

There is often a powerful urge to skip understanding and move directly to resolving. We may feel we know "the right answer" and perhaps feel some urgency in turning the yellow light to green. The client punches with a hard objection and we counterpunch, almost instinctively. With discipline and skill we can understand: the real issue, the client's criteria for resolving the issue, and what will happen if the issue is or is not resolved.

1. Understand the real issue.

The true nature of clients' concern is often unclear in how they word the yellow light. If we assume or guess at what the concern is, we may answer the wrong concern, answer it poorly, or introduce new concerns inadvertently.

For example, the client says, "I'm concerned that if we outsource to you, we'll lose control over that part of our organization."

What does "control" mean to the client? Who specifically loses control, over what? What lets them know they have, or do not have, control? What is their evidence that they are losing or gaining control? What happens when they lose control and what would be the benefit if they had more of it? How did they conclude that outsourcing would give them less control? They would not even consider outsourcing without some powerful motivation; how do the perceived advantages of outsourcing compare to the perceived loss of control? What are the constraints that have stopped them as an organization from having both the benefits of outsourcing and the desired level of control? If the control issue were resolved to their satisfaction, what would they do?

If we understand some of the foregoing, we have the opportunity in resolving to demonstrate one or more of the following:

- Outsourcing will give them more of what control means to them, rather than less.
- Outsourcing might reduce control in some areas, yet will give them more control of abilities and results that are a higher priority.
- The current level of control is not getting the results they want as an organization.
- Failure to outsource will result in even more loss of control.

By asking effective questions we can understand what it is we must resolve and gain insight on how to resolve it.

2. Understand clients' criteria for resolving the issue.

To repeat, "If we say it, it's sold; if they say it, it's gold." Clients tend to be convinced more easily, and with more conviction, if we resolve a yellow light using *their* criteria rather than our own. Client criteria are often less stringent than we fear.

> ❖ Clients tend to be convinced more easily, and with more conviction, if we resolve a yellow light using *their* criteria rather than our own.

Clients most often frame yellow lights in terms of what they *do not* like, what they *do not* want; they use the language of problems and dissatisfactions rather than resolution. It can be extremely helpful to invite them to think in terms of what they *would* like, what they *do* want, what would allow them to feel good rather than bad. The human brain, somewhat like the Internet, does search and retrieval on queries presented. If we ask it to tell us more about what is bad, it will diligently provide negative responses. Likewise, if we ask the brain for its definition of "good," we are more apt to get positive responses. Sometimes we will see a complete change in clients' facial and body expression as their brain moves from sifting through problems to the search for a solution.

A helpful phrase to elicit clients' criteria for yellow light resolution is: "What would have to happen . . . ?" We do not say, "What would *I* have to do . . . ?" or "What would *our company* have to do . . . ?" The criteria may have nothing to do with us. Resolution might be something clients and their companies have to manifest. If they need us to do something, they will say so.

Of course, we are not restricted only to "What would have to happen . . . ?" Variations include:

- "What would allow you to feel confident and comfortable that . . . ?"
- "What would you have to see or hear or experience that would allow you to . . . ?"
- "What would you have to check off in your mind and gut before . . . ?"

- "What would have to be in place before . . . ?"
- "How would you become convinced that . . . ?"

EXAMPLE 1

CLIENT: I'm not confident you have sufficient experience in our industry niche.

CONSULTANT: I appreciate your honesty. I wouldn't want to proceed without that confidence. Rather than me making what I feel are some pretty strong claims about our experience, could I ask what would have to happen from your perspective before you would be confident that our experience was completely appropriate for what you want to achieve?

EXAMPLE 2

CLIENT: I have the impression that your company focuses exclusively on technology and process and not on our people.

CONSULTANT: Wow. That's hard to hear. I appreciate your willingness to be honest. I definitely hear that focusing on your people is important to you. Rather than listening to me make a bunch of claims, what would have to be in place for you feel confident that your people are getting the focus they need and deserve?

If clients give us their criteria and we can meet them, we are more likely to turn the yellow light to green convincingly and efficiently, with nothing extra. If we cannot meet the criteria, at least we know what we are dealing with. We still have some resolution options available (see Resolve on page 151).

3. Understand what happens if we do, or do not, resolve the yellow light.

Many times consultants resolve one yellow light and then another one appears; they resolve that one and another one appears, then another one and another one. Sometimes that is not a problem; at other times it is helpful to get all the yellow lights out on the table at one time. We may discover commonalities that allow us to deal with them all at once. We may discover priorities and get further faster

> ❖ Consciously choose whether to resolve a yellow light as it appears or to collect yellow lights and address them at one time.

by dealing with the biggest issue first. We may gain momentum and rapport by resolving easy issues first and building up to the tough ones.

As a choice, we might pose a hypothetical question, either before or after asking "What would have to happen . . . ?" It could sound like the following:

- "For discussion purposes, let's say we resolve your concerns on this issue—where would we be?"
- "Hypothetically, let's say the business unit leaders do buy in—what would you do?"
- "It might be impossible. Let's say it could get done in six months— what would you decide?"
- "Just so I can understand where we are, let's say you feel very good about everything we've agreed upon with the sole exception of this one issue—what would you do?"

Doing some verbal advance scouting can help us discover a better path to resolution.

Resolve

If yellow lights exist in the client's mind, then no matter how difficult they may be, we want to bring them to the surface while we are present with the client. Once we are confident that we understand what it is we are trying to resolve, we can turn the yellow light to green, or find out that we cannot. Here are some means to do so.

FACTS AND DATA: Research on objections shows that many are simply a result of inaccurate or insufficient information. It could be as simple as clients thinking we do not provide a particular product feature even though we do. Perhaps they came to a conclusion based on inaccurate numbers or missing facts. As long as the yellow light shows up while we are still there, it can often be turned to green by simply providing what was missing or correcting inaccuracies.

Randy was working with a client whose salespeople were convinced that the primary reason they were losing sales was price. Based on that belief, they felt their company should lower prices rather than invest in more sales training. Fortunately, good win/loss data was available. Several deals were *won* when the client's price was as much as 30 percent higher than the competition's; other deals were *lost* when their prices were as much as 30 percent lower than the competition's. Furthermore, what the salespeople thought were most important to the client—price and relationships— were rated very low by the client. What was most important to the client— understanding their business challenges—was rated low in importance by the salespeople. In addition, very persuasive mathematical analysis postulated that if the salespeople made demonstrable gains in three key skill areas, sales would go up by 6 to 8 percent. The salespeople were more interested in increasing sales than in being right. With sound data available, they were eager to improve their skills rather than focus on price.

THIRD-PARTY STORIES: Most consultants have used a story about success with one client to help resolve a concern of another. They often use their own personalized version of "feel, felt, found" ("I understand how you feel, other clients have felt that way, what they found was . . ."). While the use of third-party stories is not new, the fact that they are so effective has important implications.

1. If we retain a passionate focus on helping our clients succeed in a way about which they feel good, we will have a constant supply of credible and compelling third-party stories.

2. In the Qualifying section we stressed the importance of evidence—measures that demonstrate significant improvement of clients' key performance indicators. Often the results of our products and services are difficult to measure, and it takes creativity and willingness to do so. Evidence is not only a powerful driver of additional business with current clients, it also provides credibility to third-party stories. Professionals and organizations who commit to evidence reap the rewards.

3. The persuasiveness of third-party stories increases with the similarity of the organizations and situations we compare. The weakness of third-party stories shows up when clients resist or resent the comparison; they feel they are unique. You can mitigate that by bracketing your

third-party story as follows: "I know your situation is unique, so you may or may not find this helpful . . . [Insert third party story]. What is your sense? Can you see how that might apply here as well?"

LOGIC

Human beings make predictable errors in logic and reasoning. Despite the opinion of some consultants, clients are human beings. Therefore clients, despite their opinions of themselves, make errors in logic and reasoning. We can train ourselves to recognize faulty logic. We can train ourselves to expose weaknesses in reasoning in a way that does not aggravate and alienate the client.

ANALOGIES

Clients have to sell their products and services. They get yellow lights from their customers that are similar to the ones they give to us. What do they say to their own customers to resolve these yellow lights? For instance, let's say we are entering a new market niche and the client challenges us on our experience in that niche. We could respond, "Your company has successfully entered several new market niches. When you were convinced that you had a superior solution for your prospective client, one that had worked well in other niches, yet the client challenged your direct experience in that niche, what did you say?" Clearly, we will listen closely to their response as a cue for what we might say as well.

Mahan was working on a large computer-system opportunity with the owner of a chain of retail shoe stores. The owner liked the system, yet thought other systems had the same look and feel and were less expensive. His stores sold premier-brand shoes. Mahan asked him his reason for selling premier brands rather than "knockoffs"; the latter were cheaper brands of shoes and had larger margins. He said, "Those other shoes may look similar on display, but when our customers wear them daily, they quickly look shoddy and are not at all as comfortable. We get more returns and fewer satisfied customers. And our business is about satisfied customers." By the time he finished his rant, one he had seemingly given many times before, Mahan and he both started to smile at the obvious analogy to computer systems.

METAPHORS AND STORIES

Metaphors and stories are powerful communication tools. When we hear a compelling metaphor or story, be it from a teacher, friend, author, or businessperson, it can be a bolt of lightning that brings clarity, insight, and motivation. The following can be a good investment of time:

> ❖ *Whoever Tells the Best Story Wins*: title of a book by Annette Simmons

1. Take some of the most difficult and/or frequent objections you encounter and find a metaphor that applies. You can research and select metaphors others have created or develop one of your own. Develop multiple metaphors and see how reactions to them differ.

2. Make storytelling a conscious competence; read some books and/or takes some courses; collect stories; practice your storytelling.

3. Explore experiential metaphors that people can see, do, hear, while you are with them. (For an example of a visual experiential metaphor, go to www.viscog.beckman.uiuc.edu/media/ig.html and watch the "Basketball video." How might you use this?)

REFRAMING PERCEPTIONS

In "Understand" (page 147) the authors discussed eliciting clients' criteria for resolving a yellow light. Using clients' criteria rather than our own can be very persuasive. What happens, however, if clients give us a criterion that we cannot meet? Here are three ways to fundamentally change or reframe how they relate to a given criterion.

1. Change the relative importance of the criterion.

Example: "Let's say that all the results we've been talking about are real and obtainable, that you and your customers are both big winners, that stockholders are happy, and that the only issue we can't fully resolve to your satisfaction is who owns the intellectual property rights. Would that mean you would kill the whole deal?"

2. Show that no one could meet the criterion.

Examples: "Out of curiosity, on a project of this magnitude, was any firm able to guarantee that every person working on the project would have at least eight years of experience in your industry?"

"Out of curiosity, has anybody told you they could guarantee these cost savings without having control over hiring and firing? (If so, does that seem reasonable to you?)"

3. Change the client's underlying beliefs about the criterion.

Let's say a client wants X. We do not have or do X. The client is unwilling to change the relative importance of X and feel X is obtainable from somewhere. We need to change how the client thinks about X or we may have a red light.

Here is one option:

Find the link the clients are making in their mind and either change the link or break the link.

Find the link: If they want X, determine what X equals in their mind. What does X give, or do for them?

Substitute the link: If we can give them what X equals, does that work?

Break the link: Can we show them counterindications where X does *not* equal what they want?

> ❖ With criteria you cannot meet:
>
> **1.** Change the relative importance of the criterion.
>
> **2.** Show that no one can meet the criterion.
>
> **3.** Change how the person thinks about the criterion.

Example: The client says it is important that each of the people we put on their initiative has eight or more years of in-depth experience in the clients' industry. Perhaps another firm says they can do that, yet we know *we* cannot. For us to move forward, we need to change how that client thinks about eight years of experience.

Find the link: The client has an "if . . . then" belief and has only shared part of it with us. He believes that *if* everyone on the project has eight years of experience, *then something will happen.* What is the link he has in his mind? Does eight years of experience equal better quality? Better productivity? Better project results? Faster learning curve? Lower training costs?

Substitute the link: Let's say it is the clients' belief that eight or more years experience will ensure that the project gets done on time, which is critical because of political commitments they have made. We might say to them, "I hear how important this is to you and I'd like to explore it in more depth. Let's say there were some people available, whether in our company or another, and you became convinced they were the best-suited to deliver this project on time, yet they only had three or four years of experience in your industry. Are you more concerned about the years of experience, or their ability to deliver on time?"

> ❖ If clients want X, and you cannot give them X, can you give them what X equals to them? Failing that, can you show them examples of cases where getting X will not give them what they want?

Break the link:

The following are some options for how we might break the "if . . . then" belief currently held by the client.

1. An interesting way to start breaking the link is to move in the direction opposite of the one expected. For instance, we might ask the client, "Out of curiosity, how did you pick eight years? Why not twenty years? It seems like more would be better." In describing how eight is better, or just as good a choice as twenty, the client may give arguments that would be good reasons why four is just as good a choice as eight.

2. We might inquire, "Out of curiosity, do you have people in your company who have considerably more than eight years of experience who you would not put on this time sensitive project?" ("Why would that be?")

3. "I've often heard it said of some people in our industry that although they have been here for ten years, they don't have ten years of experience—they have one year's experience repeated ten times. Have you ever found that to be the case?"

4. "With many of my clients, if I told them I was applying the thinking, processes, and technology of ten years ago to their problems of today, we'd never get hired. Even if it were from five years ago, that wouldn't cut it; everything in this industry and in this global economy is moving too rapidly. Sometimes having a team that blends knowledge of what worked in the past with those well-schooled in leading edge performance of today, gets better results than having a team composed only of people who have been doing the same things the same ways for a very long time. Would you consider using a team with more of a blend of experience?"

5. "Some of the firms that are renowned for producing great business leaders make it a practice of moving their top people not only from job to job but from industry to industry. Doing the same industry function consecutively for eight or more years would be rare for their best people. They feel that good people develop better thinking and creativity through diverse experience; they see patterns and principles that otherwise would not be apparent; they often achieve breakthroughs by applying insights from one industry to another. Even if the companies do not require the changes, many bright and capable individuals will seek out change, whether within one company or with different ones. Many of our best people have had similar career tracks. I think you would find them extremely valuable assets in meeting your delivery targets, even though they do not have eight years' experience in your industry. Would you at least be willing to consider them with an open mind?"

Unless the client changes his/her mind about what experience equals, we are dead in the water. Substituting or breaking the links in the clients' mind are good choices to have. For most consultants, it is necessary to think through some of the options in advance.

A Quick Review

For nonprice yellow lights, an effective pattern of resolution is to acknowledge, understand, resolve.

ACKNOWLEDGE

Slow down.

Appreciate.

Empathize.

Do not necessarily agree.

UNDERSTAND

Understand the real issue.

Understand how the client would resolve the issue.

❖ Seek first to understand, then to be understood.

Understand what happens if you do or do not resolve the issue.

RESOLVE

Provide facts and data.

Examine and improve logic.

Use analogies, metaphors, stories.

Reframe perceptions.

Change the relative importance of a criterion.

Show that no one can meet the criterion.

Change the client's underlying beliefs about the criterion.

Cracking the Code on Yellow Lights

One of the most challenging, fun, and rewarding experiences is helping consultants resolve their toughest yellow lights. Here are precepts the authors find helpful:

1. Intent counts more than technique: The first question we ask ourselves is, "How would turning this yellow light to green be in clients' best interests?" If there is no good answer to that question, the case is closed. If there are good answers, we keep talking.

2. Solve for the unknowns: What do clients mean by the key words and phrases they use to express the yellow light? What is their underlying concern or objective? What are their explicit and implicit "if . . .

then" beliefs? Where have they given us the "if," without clarifying the "then?" What challenges can we apply to their beliefs?

3. Create options: What are multiple choices for how to acknowledge, understand, resolve? How can we build on common interests, such as wanting the same outcomes and results? What interests do we value differently? How can conflicting interests be viewed in a different light? How can we change underlying beliefs and patterns of thinking? How have others removed similar roadblocks?

4. Prepare and practice: Many yellow lights can be predicted; we can prepare for them in advance and practice how we will acknowledge, understand, and resolve them. We can keep practicing until our reasoning is compelling and our language creates the desired reactions without raising hackles. We can practice until our responses are congruent with our personality and values.

5. Increase self-awareness: We can become more aware of the fears and desires that cause us to lose clarity and objectivity, that cause us to defend and attack rather than explore and create. We can be more willing to be "wrong," more willing to change our approach or business model, more willing to walk away when things do not make sense.

Yellow Lights on Price

The field of negotiation is rich in research, writings, and applications. To offer only a little on such a broad topic is challenging. Yet to offer nothing on price negotiation is a cop-out. Hence, here are guidelines and helpful practices, rather than an in-depth treatment.

You can't substitute good negotiation for bad selling. You should receive far less push-back on price if you have done a good job of agreeing on financial value in the Opportunity portion of qualifying. In Resources, you should have already qualified the client on the amount of investment they are willing to make to get the desired results. Hopefully, in Decisions, you have built rapport and relationships with key stakeholders; you understand their important nonprice criteria.

If clients do push back on price, *do not take it personally*. Clients have learned that often all they have to do to save their company considerable money is to say some version of "Well, we'd really like to do business with you, but your price is too high." Frequently consultants immediately drop the price, leaving clients to contemplate how stupid or fiscally irresponsible they would have been to not at least try.

Many consultants are vulnerable to price challenges because they:

- Do not establish value up-front.
- Know their prices are flexible.
- Believe that all price challenges are real.
- Believe that their counterpart knows competitive pricing.
- Dislike discussing prices.
- Focus on defending prices rather than providing results.
- Want the sale.

A Framework for Price Negotiation

ART
Aggressive
Realistic Target

NoD
No Deal

▶ Work for ART as if it were NoD

▶ Only negotiate price if it's the last issue.

▶ Offer options not ulitimatums
(prepare in advance).

▶ The first options should keep you "whole."

▶ If you offer concessions:
Concede slowly
Concede small
NEVER GIVE SOMETHING FOR NOTHING.

▶ Keep the Dialogue Open

Many clients will frequently challenge the quoted prices because:

- They lose nothing by challenging the price.
- They feel it is their responsibility.
- Sellers often give in on price.
- Value has not been created up-front.
- They do not understand what it really takes to provide the solution.

When you need to deal with price issues, the framework shown in the graphic may help.

> ❖ If clients push back on price, don't take it personally. They have been trained to do so by incompetent salespeople.

Establish Good Parameters

The final price we select should not be a shock or surprise to the client; we test a price range before we get to the final presentation. We want to choose a price that is aggressive, yet realistic—which is often a tough balance to achieve. Negotiation research shows that those who set higher targets realize greater returns. Yet if the price is too high, we lose credibility.

We must also be clear about what would constitute "no deal." "No deal" is the price below which we would rather walk away than accept the business; we have better alternatives available. Two grievous errors in negotiation are failing to reach agreement *above* the no-deal point and accepting business *below* the no-deal point. If we have not articulated our no-deal point, we are not ready to negotiate.

Many consultants concede almost too readily until they reach their no-deal point—whereupon they muster every argument available to them. Top consultants, in contrast, advocate for the aggressive, realistic target as if it were their no-deal point. If they concede, they concede in small amounts, concede slowly, and get some value exchange for each concession.

When to Deal with Price

The general rule is: only negotiate price when price is the last issue on the table. Too many consultants capitulate on price and still do not get the business. We essentially tell the client we are liars (our price was not our price) and that we are stupid (we will give something for nothing).

To find out if price is the last issue on the table, take price off the table and see what happens. We can say, "Right now we have priced this to get you the results you want. I'm not sure we can move the price without making some important

> ❖ General rule: only deal with price if price is the last issue on the table.
>
> To find out if it is the last issue, take price off the table and see what happens. If nothing happens, there is something important missing. Find out what it is.

trade-offs. Let me understand how you are thinking about this. Let's say we did agree on price; what would you do?" If they say unequivocally, "We would go with you," then price is the last issue on the table and we will talk about it. If they say anything else, then agreeing on price will not get the deal done. We might say, "Our goal is to get you a solution that truly meets your needs. It sounds like even if we agree on price something important is missing. What's missing?" Our objective is to resolve all nonprice issues first. It makes agreeing on price easier and conclusive.

Never Give Something for Nothing

Right or wrong, there are some people who will never pay the quoted price. They just can't. They need to bargain and get some concessions. Since good negotiation is a process of creating options rather than making ultimatums, concessions can make sense as long as they are not unilateral.

Price is primarily a function of scope (what we are going to do to produce the desired results), timing (how fast it will happen), and division of labor (who does what). If clients want a lower price, can they live with fewer results? If doing the project faster or slower saves us money, can clients live with different timing? Can clients take on more of the work without compromising the quality of the results? When clients want the same scope, the same timing, and the same division of labor, *then that's the price.* That is how we arrived at that price.

We should not give the same scope, timing, and division of labor for a lower price without some meaningful exchange of value. Here are some possibilities:

- We do not have to write a proposal and can pass on our cost savings to the client.
- The client provides marketing and advertising value.
- The client provides R&D collaboration; perhaps his company helps measure the effectiveness of the solution and we can write up the results in a white paper.
- The client signs up additional business now and we write down our associated business development costs.
- The client pays early and we reduce our accounts receivable costs.

When price is the last issue, examine trade-offs of price equivalents that keep you "whole."

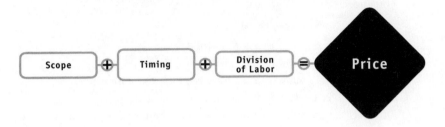

Concede Slowly, Concede in Small Amounts

Negotiation research shows that people feel just as good winning small concessions as they do large ones, as long as those concessions were difficult to achieve. We should negotiate accordingly. The trade-offs mentioned in the previous section cover small reductions in price, not large ones. Large variations in price are selling problems, not negotiating problems.

Common Price Tactics

Clients use predictable ploys to lower the price. Since clients keep using them, they must work. We do not take it personally that clients try to get the price down; hopefully they do not take it personally when we do not capitulate. We are at the last part of the buying process. All nonprice issues are resolved. They want our solution and they want us. As long as we demonstrate a little flexibility, they will likely go with us, even if their price ploys do not work.

EXAMPLE 1

CLIENT: If you do a good job on this one, there is a lot more in the pipeline.

CONSULTANT: I'm glad to hear that. If we can sign up some of that business now, I can reduce my selling costs and pass on the savings to you. How much would you like to sign up?

EXAMPLE 2

CLIENT: We need to see if you do a good job on this project first.

CONSULTANT: Great. That's reasonable and I'm confident we will do

a good job. We can leave the price where it is and agree in advance that if you sign up more business without any additional
selling costs on our part, we'll give you the discount on the future
business.

EXAMPLE 3

CLIENT: We are an important name in this industry. If you do business with us, it will win you a lot more business with others.
CONSULTANT: I certainly hope so. That is how we priced our solution. If that doesn't happen, it could be a bad miscalculation. Can
we talk a bit about what you would be willing to do in that regard?

EXAMPLE 4

CLIENT: All of our vendors are giving us a 10 percent discount.
CONSULTANT: That was made very clear to us up front and is re-
flected in the price we have given you. However, we consider that
an investment that should have a return. Once you see the value we
produce, our future bids will be at our regular price.

The authors were working on a multimillion-dollar deal for our own
company. After our presentation, the client decision makers informed us
they liked us the best, yet they wanted us to reduce our price. Their rationale was that our rates were higher than those of the partners of a well
known consulting firm. We refrained from asking, "Why don't you hire
them?" Instead, we explained that since they were looking for aggressive
results in an aggressive time frame, and that success was critical to them
both economically and politically, our price was based on bringing our "A"
team. If they were willing to compromise on the quality of people, we
could lower the price. They replied they wanted the "A" team. We responded, "That is the price it takes to get those people on board." They
agreed to move ahead.

The client's RFP (put out only *after* we had in-depth conversations with
the client), stated that payment terms were ninety days. That was unacceptable to us. In fact, we required a rather large *advance* payment. We
made it clear to the decision makers that the terms were as important to us
as the price. They said they understood. Nonetheless, several days after verbal agreement, we got a call from the head of purchasing, who explained

that the company had policies: everyone got paid in ninety days, we would not get an advance payment, and they wanted to see what our best and final price was. We explained that they already had our best and final price, and that changing the terms was a deal breaker. They told us to fax over what we were willing to do. We faxed over exactly the same agreement. The purchasing person phoned back and said, "Well, as the saying goes, you can't win if you don't try. If that is the best you can do, let's move ahead." We did not take it personally that they tried (though it was tempting), and they did not seem to take it personally that we did not comply.

Next Steps and Agenda

MEETING PLAN

End in Mind
Key Beliefs
Proof/Action
Questions
Yellow Lights
Next Steps
Agenda

Next Steps

If the decision we enable is *not* the final decision, we should confirm the remaining steps in the decision grid. We and the client should stay mutually aware of how we are jointly moving forward. If the decision we enable *is* the final decision, see "Results" on page 167.

Be prepared to ask for, or to offer next steps at the end of every meeting.

Agenda

Organize the End in Mind and key beliefs into an agenda. If at all possible, test the agenda with clients before the meeting. Invite them to add, modify, or delete. When the client agrees on the agenda in advance, you will be more effective in the meeting and will be more likely to enable a decision.

A Quick Review of the Meeting Plan

Start with the End in Mind: What do you want clients to comfortably and confidently say, do, or decide at the end of the meeting? Gain agreement on the End in Mind either before, or at the beginning of the meeting.

Ask clients (and yourself) what they would have to resolve, intellectually and emotionally, before they would be able and willing to decide on the End in Mind (key beliefs).

For each key belief, provide proof or propose action to address that belief. Answer any client questions, making sure to answer the real question. Ask any questions you need or want to ask.

For each key belief, find out if clients have resolved the belief to their satisfaction. If all lights are green, proceed to the next belief. If there are yellow lights, acknowledge, understand, and resolve the best you can. Either address each yellow light as it appears, or create a list of the yellow lights to address before the end of the meeting.

When you have covered the key beliefs, ask for the End in Mind. If there are remaining yellow lights, turn them to green the best you can. If something else needs to happen before the decision is made, make sure you understand exactly what is needed, how it is important, and what will happen if you provide it. If "nothing will happen" when you provide it, then something is missing; find out what it is before you leave, and revisit what should happen next.

If the decision is an interim decision rather than a final one, make sure everyone agrees on *all* the next steps; each step should have a go/no go decision, a date, and should specify the people involved.

Create an agenda that lays out the End in Mind and the path for getting there. Gain agreement from the client on the agenda before the meeting if at all possible. Make changes, if appropriate, so that everyone knows where they are going and how they will get there.

RESULTS

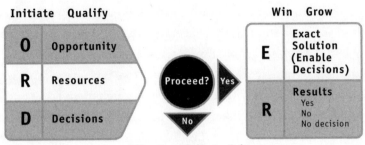

After we present our solution, clients will respond in one of three ways. They could say, "Yes, let's do it." They could say, "No, thank you." They could "not decide." No matter what the clients choose, there are actions we can take that will help create a positive relationship moving forward.

"Yes, Let's Do It."

The ability to deliver a solution that truly meets the client's needs develops far more sales than any of our selling activities. Happy clients not only give us more business themselves, they are the source of vital references. The classic error of consultants is to get the business and then move on. They leave behind more business than whatever they move on to.

Studies show that profitability is most affected by account retention, account expansion, and being the primary provider of services in an account. To ensure that we get the benefits from helping our client succeed over the long term, consider the following:

1. Turn future yellow lights to green—now.

As much as we have been talking about a solution that exactly meets clients' needs, no solution is exact. No implementation of a complex product or service is perfect. Both we and clients can predict events that may inhibit success. It can be helpful to talk about those events now, when the relationship is strong and positive, rather than when the events occur and the relationship is stressed. We might say, "Out of curiosity, have you ever experienced an installation of this scale that went absolutely perfectly?" When they say no, we can continue, "And neither have we. Both of us begin with an expectation that all will go well and both of us know some likely challenges we will face along the way. We have found it helpful to talk through some of those potential challenges in advance. Perhaps we can prevent them. If we can't, having talked about what to do in advance will help us move through them faster and easier if they do occur. Would that be a useful conversation for us to have?"

Should we choose to have this discussion, let clients get out their list of challenges first, and then talk about them: "So if that happens, what should we do?" or, "How would you like to avoid that?" or, "What would have to happen to make you comfortable with that?"

Then we give *our* list. We might talk about change of scope, their failure to meet commitments on time, changes in personnel, missed deadlines, etc. Set up lines of good communication now; if something occurs, we will know how to talk about it effectively, and we are not caught up in the emotions and fears of the moment.

This process is sometimes called preemptive negotiation. It is a powerful choice and one that is underutilized.

2. Ensure a smooth transition from "sales" to delivery.

We have invested a lot of time understanding the issues, evidence, impact, context, and constraints. It is critical that we work closely with the implementers of the solution to ensure that what they purchased is what they get.

3. Measure results.

Maintain the pressure on your company and clients to measure results. This is both challenging and important. Have you ever seen a new client executive look at expenditures for your company and say, "Hey, we've spent a lot of money with these people. What do we have to show for it?" We want to have good answers for that question.

> ❖ If we don't treat current clients like prospective clients, they will become former clients.

4. Establish an account management strategy.

We should always be thinking, "How

can I help this client succeed?" If we retain and magnify that focus, there will be multiple opportunities to pursue. We can use the tools in the Initiating section to bring new ideas to current clients, and do so in a way that the client feels good about.

"No, Thank You."

Almost all consultants know the value of finding out the real reasons we won or lost a deal. Yet few get accurate feedback on a consistent basis. Most win/loss studies are based on stated importance—what clients say made a difference to them. In addition, we can use mathematical analysis to infer from stated importance the specific attributes and behaviors most correlated to success or failure. We can predict that a measurable increase in those characteristics will produce a specific percentage increase in sales. This gives us the ability to target our training and calibrate results. It allows us to focus more and execute better.

Many times, the reasons we think we have won or lost are not what the client was thinking or feeling.

No Decision

Try as we might to enable a decision, some clients will not decide. They will not say yes or no. After a certain amount of time for reasonable contemplation, it is helpful to say to the client, "Either this is a good investment and every day that you don't proceed you are losing money, or it is not a good investment, and keeping it alive wastes time and energy. Let's figure out a series of steps we can take together, at the end of which, you would feel comfortable saying either yes or no—and "no" is perfectly okay."

We can live with yes; we can live with no; the interminable maybes are black holes. If it makes sense, let's do it. If it does not make sense, let's move on.

CHAPTER SEVEN

INITIATING NEW OPPORTUNITIES

Can we say it? Cold-calling sucks.

Some salespeople make a hundred cold calls, out of which they might generate ten appointments, and from them, one or two sales. They experience massive rejection before getting any reward. Others never touch a telephone. They send an onslaught of e-mails hoping that some may escape the delete button. They may avoid direct rejection, yet the results are equally dismal.

It is a painful process for clients as well. They get inundated with cold calls and electronic contacts from people who have no understanding of them or their business. It is aggravating and annoying. The default response is, "Go away. I don't want any." "Remove me from your distribution list."

Yet, if we are skilled at initiating new opportunities, we have a chance at freeing ourselves. We can free ourselves *from* chasing deals in the pipeline that don't make sense. We can free ourselves *to* create new business whenever we want. We are in charge of our sales destiny; no matter what else is happening around us, we can consistently start with nothing and end up with good, profitable business.

So how do we generate new business in a way that avoids agony and produces good results? The real secret is to get people to call us. Rather than spend all of our time reaching out to potential clients, we cause them to "reach in" to us. When someone initiates a call to us, they do so for a reason. They have some idea that what we do may be of help. We can move off the solution and structure the conversation. And that conversation tends to flow much more easily.

Getting potential clients to call us does not need to be merely a fortuitous event. We can make it happen on purpose by developing a personal marketing and network plan that will cause people to call us on a regular basis. Such plans welcome leads generated by our company, yet do not rely on them. This ability is such a difference maker, it warrants a book in itself. In Appendix Three the authors offer some thoughts to get you started. If what you encounter there resonates and you would like to explore it further, give us a call and we'll see if we can help. And let's not forget—if we concentrate on helping clients succeed, our reputation often does our cold-calling for us.

Most of us, nonetheless, will want to initiate new business with existing and potential clients who have not had the insight or good fortune to call us. That is the subject of this section.

The initiating process allows both us and the client to answer the question, "Should we be talking?" The initiating phase begins when we first identify a prospect and continues until the prospect says either, "This sounds interesting; I would like to pursue this idea," or, "No, thank you." That answer can happen in the initial phone call, or it can take a few meetings. When we and the prospect feel there is something worth talking about, we move into qualifying.

Here is the "Initiating New Opportunities" approach at a glance:

1. Prioritize: Do fewer; do them better.
2. Prepare: Develop in-depth knowledge of the company and people you will call on. Prepare client oriented communications.
3. Personalize: NO COLD CALLS! Get a referral to the person you want to see.
4. Practice: Rehearse what you will say and how you will say it. Rehearse your responses to potential questions and yellow lights.
5. Pre-position: Get agreement in advance for what will be a good use of time.

PRIORITIZE: DO FEWER, DO THEM BETTER

We have all heard it—sales is a numbers game. Just make more calls and you will sell more. If that approach is working for you, keep doing it. The authors' experience is that often the opposite is true. When we focus on increasing low-probability activities such as cold calls, we just do more of something that doesn't work. The more calls we try to cram into the available time, the less attention goes into each call. As quality decreases, rejections increase. As rejections increase, we make more calls. This is not a good system.

When we do fewer calls, and do them better, we make more sales and enjoy our profession a lot more. This shift in thinking is a game changer. It is fundamental to increasing the success and satisfaction of both buyers and sellers. Yet it can be a difficult transition for business owners and sales professionals who are used to managing quantity rather than quality. Perhaps that is because they assume some of the people they manage want to do fewer calls, without doing them better.

Most consultants, even those selling big-ticket engagements, have dozens to hundreds of potential clients and invest similar energy in all of them. Remember, "He who defends everything, defends nothing." Instead, the authors recommend that you choose your top *five* prospects and invest 95 percent of your prospecting energy in those opportunities. When you take one prospect off the focused priority list, put a new one on; periodically review the list. Over time, you will work your way through many potential clients; however at any given moment only five will get your concentrated attention.

> ❖ The 80/20 rule doesn't go far enough. Apply the 95/5 rule.

The authors were engaged by a business process outsourcing firm to help them enter a new market and approach their first prospects. We will call them We-Do-It, and use their experience as a continuing example throughout the Initiating section. We-Do-It had a list of more than one hundred potential clients. We worked with them to prioritize their list. Criteria included:

- Likelihood of getting a referral to the CEO or CFO
- Prestige of their name as a reference
- Fit of our solution to the client's situation
- Potential economic return

We used the criteria to narrow the list from 100 potentials to 5 high-probability ones. Before we started working with them, We-Do-It was headed down the path of investing its sales and marketing budget in all 100 potentials. We instead invested the same resources in the 5 we selected. After some additional investigation, we narrowed the list to 3 and have since won business with all of them. Our client has begun this process again with the next 5 potentials: focus, execute, succeed, repeat.

PREPARE

The way many consultants use their preparation time is upside down. Consultants often invest significant resources in the final proposal or oral presentation, but spend little time honing the initial approach. Yet many buyers make their buying decision early in the process, often based on emotion and instinct, even though they may not *give* their decision until much later. Much of the sales process merely allows them to justify what they decided early on. Nowhere in the sales process do a few minutes of dialogue more quickly determine whether we continue or end our relationship, than the initial interaction. A negative first encounter could eliminate, or substantially postpone, revenue from that client. A positive beginning increases the success rate of current ideas and makes it more likely that future ideas will get an audience.

Two critical preparation elements are, one, a business case hypothesis and, two, a meeting plan. The business case hypothesis articulates reasons why mutual exploration with the client might make sense; we will test that hypothesis with the client. The Meeting Plan is the same as described in detail in the previous chapter on winning; it is used here for the initial calls rather than the concluding presentation.

The Business Case Hypothesis

There are three parts to the business case hypothesis: the client's situation, our solution, and the reasons adopting that solution might make sense.

By focusing on fewer opportunities, we can do more thorough research on the client's situation and develop a hypothesis that is likely to resonate with the prospective client. There are two scenarios to consider. Scenario One is when we have good data about the prospect's business. This is most likely in the case of existing clients, publicly traded companies, those in the news, and private companies where we have information from a third party or through direct experience. Scenario Two is when detailed information about the prospect's business is either unavailable or too difficult to get.

When conducting research for companies in Scenario One, we want to learn the following:

Context: What issues and trends are affecting the client's industry? What are the clients key strategies and initiatives that affect everything it does?

Issues: What business problems or results does the client have that are addressed by our solution?

Evidence: What data and/or opinions suggest something needs to change?

Impact: What are the probable financial and intangible consequences of the issues?

Constraints: What has stopped or might stop the client from addressing the issues?

These should all seem familiar. They are from the Opportunity checklist described in the qualifying section.

Scenario One:

One of We-Do-It's top three prospects was a company that we will refer to as NewLogo. NewLogo was a public company and a tremendous amount of data was available. In addition to reviewing data, we also talked with the referral source who knew the CFO well. We discovered that the CFO of NewLogo was very open to new ideas, and was the principal decision maker in the company for operating issues addressed by the We-Do-It solution. We decided to make the CFO our entry point, and we analyzed our research through a filter of what would be relevant to the CFO.

To NewLogo, the estimated impact of the relevant issues was between 2 to 7 percent of a segment of their revenue. We used 5 percent as a working number. That translated into about $36 million per year.

When we explored constraints (What might prevent NewLogo from addressing the issues?), we came up with the following:

1. Disbelief that "anyone" could address such a complex problem.
2. Time and people resources are scarce and there may be areas to concentrate on that would produce higher returns.
3. If an outside firm did address the problem, it might reflect poorly on internal resources who have defended the "that's the way it is" and "it costs more to fix than it is worth" position.

Scenario Two

We may have prospects who meet some basic qualification criteria, yet detailed information about their business is either unavailable or too difficult to get.

In these scenarios we create a "presumed" business case hypothesis. We look at companies in the industry or market niche that most closely resemble our prospect. We organize what we believe to be true about these *types* of companies, realizing that only good inquiry will reveal whether or not they apply to our prospect.

To build a presumed business case, it is helpful to interview ourselves in the same way we would interview a client:

1. A helpful place to start is to "move off" our own solution. We brainstorm a list of all the problems our solution could solve, and/or results it could create, for clients similar to the prospective client.

> ❖ We should move off our own solution.

2. We organize the list into themes (groups of issues) and/or likely priorities.

3. We select from the list those themes or priorities that have the greatest potential impact.

4. We examine the types of evidence that would prove or disprove the existence of those issues. We calculate the potential impact of those issues to a company of a particular size.

5. We think through reasons that the companies might not successfully address these issues, as well as why they might not even consider some new options.

6. We look at the overall context in which these companies exist; we reason about the people and functions in these companies that would be affected by the issues and by the implementation of our solution.

All of this should sound familiar. We are qualifying our own solution, looking at issues, evidence, impact, constraints, and context.

You might want to pull out your computer or a pad of paper and do the following exercise. Interview yourself about your own company's solution. We will use a generic Customer Relationship Management (CRM) software application for our example.

Step One: Ask yourself, what are all the problems (or results) that would have to exist in your prospect's company before key people there would be excited to talk about your solution? If they do not care about the problems or results your solution resolves, they will not care about your solution. No pain, no gain, no opportunity.

A partial list for the CRM example might look like the accompanying chart.

Problem or Result	Evidence	Impact
Missed sales goals		
Lack information about key customers		
Want a better coverage model		

Problem or Result	Evidence	Impact
Takes too long for new salespeople to be productive		
Need one place to go for customer information		
Want to improve and personalize the customer experience		
Need to improve sales productivity		
Poor forecasting ability		

Step Two: For each issue, what evidence does, or might, exist that would indicate a potential problem or opportunity? Where would we get that evidence?

Step Three: What might be the financial impact of this issue for companies the size of your prospect? You won't know specifically, yet you can get an order of magnitude.

The CRM example for these steps might look like the accompanying table.

Problem or Result	Evidence	Impact
Missed sales goals	Inconsistent ability to hit quarterly sales goals: by product, by team, or by individual	Dollars of sales, margins, profits
Lack information about key customers	It takes too long to respond to customer inquiries. Unable to cross and up-sell at point of sale	Dollars of: initial sales, additional items, lifetime revenue
Want a better coverage model	Some reps have too many prospects, some too few	Dollars of missed sales, low dollars sold per rep, high sales costs
Takes too long for new salespeople to be productive	Time from hiring to working is too long; productivity of new reps low	Training costs too high; low dollars per rep for new reps; slow sales growth

Problem or Result	Evidence	Impact
Need one place to go for customer information	Multiple systems or spreadsheets with often conflicting data	High systems costs; high support costs; low revenue per customer
Want to improve and personalize the customer experience	Not able to differentiate by customer; large number of customer complaints	Dollars and margin per customer; lifetime customer revenue
Need to improve sales productivity	Too few salespeople hit quota; key sales metrics are at or worse than industry average	Sales costs too high; can't calculate what improved productivity would bring to bottom line
Poor forecasting ability	Significant gaps between expectations and actual performance	Either employee costs high or sales results too low

We might organize the above list into three "themes":

1. Sales volume issues: too-little or too-slow revenue (and margin) growth
2. Sales productivity issues: per salesperson cost and performance metrics need improvement
3. Sales information issues: poor availability and quality of customer information hurting per-customer performance

Step four: Think through reasons companies might not successfully address these issues, as well as why they might not even consider some new options. For CRM that might include:

- They have tried CRM before and had a bad experience.
- They don't think their people will use CRM or that using it will be a waste of the salespeople's time.
- They think their current system is good enough.
- Money is tight. They can't afford a new investment.

And so on.

Step five: Look at the overall context in which these companies exist. Think about the people and functions in these companies that would be affected by the issues, and by the implementation of our solution.

We may want to call on people in the organization beyond our normal contacts. For instance, if for CRM we generally call on the head of sales, we might additionally want to call on the CFO or CEO or other people directly affected by the presumed issues.

At the end of our "move off the solution" exercise, we should be able to talk about our solution in terms of the *problems it solves and the results it produces,* rather than its features and benefits. We should be able to talk about those issues in terms of specific evidence and impact. If clients do not care about the problems or results our solution addresses, they will not care about the solution.

The Meeting Plan

Once we have developed our business case hypothesis, we are ready to create a first draft of a Meeting Plan. The same Meeting Plan introduced earlier for final presentations will be used here for an initial call.

MEETING PLAN

End in Mind	What do we want the client to say, do, decide at the end of the meeting? How will we gain agreement to the EIM before or at the beginning of the meeting?
Key Beliefs	What will the client likely need to believe, intellectually and emotionally, to comfortably decide on the EIM?
Proof/Action	What proof or proposed action will we provide to address the key beliefs?
Questions	What would we most like to know from the client? How will we ask? What questions is the client likely to ask? How will we respond?

Yellow Lights	What reasons might the client have for not deciding or deciding not in our favor (stalls, doubts, concerns, objections)?
Next Steps	What next steps, if any, should we be prepared to offer?
Agenda	What is a concise agenda that integrates all of the above? How can we best gain agreement to the agenda?

THE END IN MIND

In this early stage of the sales cycle we are not trying to sell anything! We simply want to decide if spending time discussing a potential business opportunity makes sense—or not. Our End in Mind is—*should we be talking?*

KEY BELIEFS

There are some common beliefs that the client would likely have to hold before they would agree that it would make sense for us to talk. They might include:

- We have something worth talking about.
- It would be enjoyable (or at least not painful) to have the meeting.
- The clients' time will be used well.

There may be others; addressing these three successfully should get us far down the path.

For example, the key beliefs that We-Do-It developed for NewLogo were:

1. There is something worth finding.
   (Certain NewLogo stakeholders felt that they were running a tight ship and that the proposed initiative would not find enough results to make it worthwhile. Unless this belief was resolved, everything else was moot.)
2. The investment of time is appropriate and available.
   (Even if there were something worth finding, NewLogo still had to invest their people's time and that time was scarce.)

3. The economics make sense.

(NewLogo needed to believe that the fee arrangement was reasonable.)

For the Scenario Two CRM example, prospect clients would need to believe they had significant pain or gain in relation to sales volume, salesperson productivity, or pertinent sales information. They would need belief, or at least open-mindedness, that CRM could help. And it would aid the cause if they believed our company was a proven CRM solution provider.

PROOF/ACTION

For both scenarios, we will use our referral person and our preparation of the business case hypothesis to substantiate that there is something worth talking about.

We will carefully craft our language and approach to keep the encounter enjoyable.

We will use the Meeting Plan to make good use of time.

We will always be prepared to let the client do most of the talking if and when they want to do so.

QUESTIONS

On the first call or meeting, we come prepared to suggest some possible reasons we should be talking. However, a major goal is to move from advocacy of our hypothesis to inquiry about the client's perceptions and feelings. Even though *we* initiated the meeting, we want to ask questions that encourage *the client* to do most of the talking.

Some generic examples might be:

- "I really appreciate the time we have to spend together today. I know time is valuable, and I want to make sure that whatever we discuss is as relevant as possible. If we were only able to talk about one, two, or three key issues (around the topic of interest) that would make this a good use of your time, what would you like to make sure we cover?"
- "One of the benefits I believe we bring to the table is tying our solution to your key business strategies and objectives. Would you feel

comfortable starting out our conversation talking at a high level about what you see as the top three to five business challenges or opportunities you face over the next one to two years?"

For the Scenario Two CRM example, we might prepare a question such as:

"I don't know how it is with you—I know when I'm talking to other VPs of sales about CRM systems, three things I keep hearing are:

1. They have sales volume issues—they aren't getting the growth that is needed and expected.
2. They have salesperson productivity issues—there are key performance measures that need to improve.
3. They have sales information issues—there is key customer information that is not available or takes too long to get and it is hurting revenue per customer.

Are any of those an issue for you as well?"

If clients say they have any one, or all of the issues, we can inquire further about evidence, impact, context, and constraints. If they have none of those issues, we can follow up with, "Great. Glad to hear it. Out of curiosity, what *are* some of the issues you face around improving sales performance?"

In the We-Do-It example, the questions prepared in advance were:

1. We want to ask
   a. What assets if any do you suspect are problematic?
   b. How would you size the potential—assuming it could be captured?
   c. What might prevent the company from trying a new approach?
2. We expect from them
   a. We have tried to address this ourselves and concluded that it would cost more to solve the problem than the size of the problem itself. How could you do it if we couldn't?
   b. Where have you done this successfully before?

When asking questions, our emphasis is on importance, not completeness. Randy was a customer in a first meeting with a vendor whom he had never met. The salesperson handed him a list of questions. There were fifty-three questions for a one-hour meeting. Ridiculous was not the only word that came to mind. If we could ask only three to five questions, and the client would answer them thoroughly, what would they be?

In addition to the questions we want to ask are the questions we expect from the client. Many of the questions clients will ask us are predictable. It serves us well to have thought about the answers in advance.

Initial client calls are more successful when the client does most of the talking. Yet when the client asks questions, most consultants answer with in-depth responses. The client follows up with more questions, the consultant responds, and by the end of the meeting time the client has talked little. It can benefit us greatly if we practice the art of redirection—answering a question with a question. Used selectively, skillful redirection will allow the client to do more talking than would otherwise occur; it will keep the focus on the client rather than the consultant.

Yellow Lights

A yellow light is a signal that the client will not decide at all, or will not decide in our favor. At this initial stage of the sales cycle, all we are asking is should we be talking? Yellow lights we might encounter here include:

1. "I'm busy. Call me later."
Response: "I would be happy to. May I give you a quick overview of what we might discuss and you can decide if you even want me to call back? If it is not of interest, I don't want to waste your time."

2. "I am happy with our current partner."
Response: "That's good to hear. In the interest of continuous improvement, is there anything that your current partner doesn't do, or do well, that might be worth exploring? No is an okay answer."

3. "I am not interested."
Response: "Thanks for being direct. Before we go, just out of curiosity, are you not interested because you are not experiencing these

issues? Am I calling at a bad time? Or is it because you have these issues covered?"

For We-Do-It, the yellow lights we prepared for were:

1. We don't have time to invest in this.
2. It will take too long to get the data.
3. We are busy, and having your people here would be a distraction to what we really need to address.

For the CRM example we would work through responses to the most common or difficult yellow lights. The ones we predicted before were:

- They have tried CRM before and had a bad experience.
- They don't think their people will use CRM or that using it will waste the salespeople's time.
- They think their current system is good enough.
- Money is tight. They can't afford a new investment.

Next Steps

The outcome of initiating is to answer the question, "Should we be talking?" If we and the client conclude there is something worth pursuing, we should be ready to offer a few steps that we could take *together,* that would allow us to mutually conclude whether the idea makes sense and should be implemented, or that it does not because better options are available. Ideally, each step is relatively low risk and a low investment for both parties. If, and only if, everything keeps making sense do we continue down the path.

We always look for opportunities to increase the speed of the sales cycle. What steps could be condensed? What are the things that, if accomplished before our first meeting or next call, would make the sales cycle shorter for both parties? A short sales cycle is in clients' best interest, as well as our own. They are the ones who will get the ultimate business benefit, the sooner the better. They hate to waste time. Getting to yes or no efficiently serves everyone. Here are some helpful hints:

1. Give clients homework. Ask them to provide necessary information in advance.
2. Before a meeting, interview the people who will attend the meeting. Find out what will make the meeting a good use of their time.
3. Gain agreement on the End in Mind and key beliefs before the meeting (see Pre-positioning Meetings for Success on page 196).

The accompanying table is an example of Next Steps for We-Do-It.

Steps	Decisions	When	Who	Criteria
Meet with the finance team	Are they experiencing the problem? .			
Validate business case	Is the problem significant enough to matter?			
Meet with the controller	Do the economics make sense? Are internal resources available?			
Formal proposal	Go or no/go			

We-Do-It was able to condense all four steps into *one* meeting. Both companies were willing to do sufficient homework and come to the meeting prepared to make a decision.

An example of possible next steps for a Scenario Two situation is shown in the following table.

Steps	Decisions	When	Who	Criteria
Meet with initial client person	Is there sufficient interest to keep talking?			

Steps	Decisions	When	Who	Criteria
Validate business case	Compelling and believable or not?			
Interview key stakeholders	Do we understand issues and criteria from their perspective? Any fatal flaws? Qualify Resources			
"What . . . if" oral presentation	Do we have a solution that meets the needs?			
Formal proposal	Go or no/go			

AGENDA

The last preparation element of the Meeting Plan is the agenda. If this is a first call, an agenda isn't necessary. However if during your first call you and the client decide that it makes sense to meet or talk again, framing out an agenda for that meeting is helpful.

Typically, agendas read like this:

1. Introductions
2. Our company overview
3. Our company's products/services/methodologies
4. Clients our company has worked with
5. Next steps

Does this look familiar?

Here is an example of the meeting agenda for NewLogo.

Meeting Purpose: To decide if a revenue transaction analysis makes sense or not.

AGENDA

Is there something worth finding? We have analyzed revenue related errors. We would like to present our thinking. We invite your team to add their perspective. If we agree there is something worth finding, we can discuss the recovery process and approach.

Is the necessary investment of time appropriate and feasible? The potential return requires an investment of your staff's time. We believe that we have minimized this investment. We will present how we manage the engagement and how much time we need from your staff so that you can decide if the investment makes sense.

Do the economics make sense? We offer two fee arrangements. Option one is value based where we share in the returns we produce. Option two is time and materials. Both arrangements depend on variables we can discuss during the meeting. Before we conclude the meeting, you will understand our fees and can decide whether or not they make sense.

Decide: Should we conduct a revenue transaction analysis?

This agenda is specific, client-centered, and focused on a path that would enable a decision, one way or the other.

PERSONALIZE: NO COLD CALLS!
GET A REFERRAL TO THE CLIENT.

One research study revealed that the odds of a business executive agreeing to talk with you are:

> ❖ When it comes to gaining appointments with prospective clients, are you getting colder or warmer?

84 percent if referred by a person she knows inside her company.

44 percent if referred by a person she knows outside her company.

44 percent if you connect with her outside of her office, such as at a conference or social gathering.

Please compare those numbers to the percentage of time prospective clients take your cold calls, whether you have sent them a letter in advance or not.

When we focus on fewer opportunities, we can commit to getting a referral—either someone calls the prospect on our behalf, or allows us to use their name when we call. Some consultants feel it is unrealistic or impractical to get referrals. Yet Internet research and social networking technology have revolutionized the ability to make connections. When we research potential companies, we also do in-depth research on the people we will call on. Those people have a web of connections, past and present. Somewhere, somehow, we have a link to these people. The authors (and the people they work with directly) get a referral to prospective clients every time—even in industries where we start without knowing a single person—and are calling on top level executives. Sometimes it takes us months to get a referral; we would rather wait until we get one than make a low-percentage cold call.

One obvious key to always having a referral is to always engage in actively developing them. Referrals come easily when we are committed to helping clients succeed in a way they feel good about. Today's successful and happy clients are tomorrow's referrals. Many salespeople leave an account immediately after it is sold. When they do this they are leaving more than just the account behind; they are leaving business that is likely more valuable than the potential project they are trying to move on to.

> ❖ The single largest determinant of profitability is account retention. . . . We have found that many sales forces are overly focused on attracting new accounts and neglect the highly profitable retention opportunities. They are hunters not gatherers. Yet gathering is often more efficient, if less exciting.   —*Benson Shapiro* et al., Harvard Business Review

Outside of our client base, every person we meet is a potential referral. Potential referrals tend to fall into three categories: people who know us well, people *we* know, and people we know of. Each of these sources has its pros and cons.

Source	Pros	Cons
Family, friends, close business associates	Willingness strong	Limited connections to priority prospects
People we know: friends of friends, colleagues, clients, professional contacts	Willingness reasonable	Action tends to be low
People we know of: the outer network of the people we know; people we identify who are close to the prospective client yet with a weak connection to us	May have strong connection to priority prospects	Willingness suspect

People who know and trust us are our best referral sources, but often this group is small relative to the other two and may not have a lot of contacts in our target market. The second source of referrals is accessible and often has the contacts we need. They are also usually agreeable to helping us. Yet often, when we call to ask for their help, they agree (because they are polite) and then nothing happens. We need to make these people confident about referring us to their personal or professional contacts. Source three has a lot of contacts, yet they are people who are harder to connect with and less motivated to help. We need to make it worthwhile and easy for them to participate.

We get more referrals from sources two and three when we:

1. Treat the call asking for a referral with the same, if not more, care and attention as when calling the client.
2. Make it easy for the referral person to take action.

The End in Mind for a referral is—Are you ready?—whether or not he or she would feel comfortable giving us a referral. The key is making "no" be an okay answer. We only want them to do it if they are willing. We will make it easy for them to say no, which, paradoxically, usually makes it more likely they will say yes.

After some small-talk and catching up, we might say:

"Hey, John—I'm calling to ask for a possible favor. I've been research-ing XYZ and I have reason to believe what we do might be of interest to them. I'm looking for a meeting with Susan Ellsbury. I think you might know her or know someone who does. Does her name ring a bell?" (If yes . . .) "I'm not at all assuming you want to give me a referral or that you should. I was hoping I could just give you a quick overview of what I had in mind and you could decide what you would like to do. I wouldn't want you to do anything you weren't completely comfortable with. Do you have a few minutes to hear me out?"

Because we have done our research and our draft of a meeting plan, we *try out with the referral the reasoning we will give to the prospective client.* Many good things result. First, we get to experience a trial run of what we will say, in a low-risk environment. Second, the person who is putting his or her good name on the line can choose whether or not to refer us, with good knowledge of what is about to happen. Third, our referral may help refine our thinking. Fourth, our referral may suggest other people we might want to talk with.

If the referral is going to call on our behalf, rather than just allow us to use his or her name, it may be helpful to provide a suggested script of how to approach the call, or to at least walk through it. The referral is unlikely to give it as much thought as we have. People sometimes appreciate having a structure for the call. We obviously don't expect them to read it verbatim. It might look like this:

"I am writing/calling regarding introducing you to John Smith. I wouldn't think of passing on his name unless I had some reason to believe that what he does could have some meaningful applications to you and your business. John is expert in automating operations and works with manufacturing firms like yours that have outgrown their existing manu-facturing and distribution platform and are looking to go in a new direc-tion. I've heard of some good measurable results coming out of his work. Whether they would apply to you or not, I don't know. That would be the reason for the call. It might be worth your while to talk with John. I have found him to be honest and straightforward. When John asked for my help, he made it clear he'll keep the call short if you two find there isn't any good reason to talk. Would you be okay with a short introductory chat? If so, I will have him call you. If not, I will let him know."

While you will word the script differently, note that it covers the three common beliefs:

1. There is something worthwhile to talk about.
2. It will be enjoyable rather than painful.
3. Your time will be respected.

Here is Randy's story of how referrals were created for We-Do-It:

We-Do-It's target companies were chosen in part because of the high likelihood of getting a referral. The referral to the first company was relatively easy—it was a referral from a relative of a We-Do-It executive (source 1).

For the second target, I had a friend who worked in the sales department of a large multinational enterprise (source 2). I contacted him and said, "We're doing some work for We-Do-It and one of our prospects is XYZ. In doing a little research, we noticed that your company has an investment in XYZ. Do you know anyone there?" He replied, "No, I don't, but a good friend of mine, Bill, heads our investment department and I'm sure he knows all the key players at XYZ. I'll have him call you." Later that day Bill called (source 3). He asked what We-Do-It did, and who we wanted to talk to. When we told him we wanted to talk with the CFO, he suggested that the CEO was more appropriate and that he would call him and set it up.

While this sounded great it felt like it could be a polite do-nothing. My reply went something like this: "I appreciate your willingness to set that up and at the same time I want to make sure that we have the right fit and are positioned well with the CEO from the start. If you would be willing, could I buy you lunch next week? You could meet us, we will give you more details about the kinds of problems we solve, and the results we help produce, and then you can decide if it still makes sense to set that meeting up." He agreed, and the following week we met.

We ended up meeting in his office instead of having lunch; we were there for two hours discussing our business. Our source took such an interest he told us about his business and even gave us a tour of the facility. By the end of this time, he knew quite a bit about our business and could represent and position us well to the CEO. He agreed to call the CEO and get us an appointment. On the walk from his office to the lobby on our way out he said, "I like your style and business model. If things go well with XYZ I know the CEOs at [two other major players on our list] and I would be happy to set you up there as well.

We-Do-It just completed a successful engagement with XYZ. What made the difference in this situation was treating the referral source that same way I would treat a client.

The third prospect was NewLogo. One of the partners at We-Do-It had a friend that supposedly knew some people at NewLogo; we will call him Nick. We contacted Nick and shared what we were doing and asked if he knew how we could best connect with NewLogo. He said that he knew several people there and was good friends with the CFO. He said that he would think about helping us and let us know.

A few days later our source called and said that he had arranged a lunch meeting between him, us, and the CFO of NewLogo. The meeting was a long plane ride away, yet it sounded like a great opportunity. We decided to ask our referral source to arrange a phone call with the CFO so that we could test our business case hypothesis and talk through an agenda for our lunch meeting. He reluctantly agreed to set up a call; he couldn't understand why we wanted a phone call since we were already going to have a meeting. This is what happened.

NICK: Hello, William, I have Melissa [We-Do-It partner] on the line and we want to talk with you about our lunch meeting next week.

WILLIAM: Okay—what do you need?

MELISSA: I appreciate you agreeing to have lunch, and I don't want you to invest your time just to find out if what we might help you with is of interest, and then need another meeting to look at the details. It seems like one meeting would be better than two. Could I quickly share with you what we are thinking? Then we can decide if meeting for lunch would make sense or if some other choice would be a better investment of your time.

WILLIAM: Sure, what are you thinking?

MELISSA: As Nick shared with you, we help companies like yours get more out of their revenue cycle by analyzing and correcting erroneous transactions. We did some preliminary analysis and based on the public data that was available—and I realize that is incomplete—it appears as though there might be as much as $36,000,000 in recoverable revenue, all of which could drop to your bottom line.

WILLIAM: That's impossible. The number is nowhere near that big.

MELISSA: I expected that to be the case as I only have an outside perspective. What do you think is a more realistic number?

WILLIAM: I don't know, but if it were even $3,000,000 I would want to recover it.

MELISSA: The only way we would know what is possible would be to get some data and review it with your team. Do you think it would make sense to do that?

WILLIAM: Sure. We run a tight operation and I want to make sure that we collect every dollar that we are due.

MELISSA: Well, you know your organization better than I do. Who needs to participate and how should we arrange the meeting?

WILLIAM: You would need to talk with our revenue auditor and our controller. Let's plan to meet as a group before lunch.

MELISSA: That would be great. Can we develop the agenda together for our meeting?

WILLIAM: "That's fine. Send me an e-mail and I'll let you know what I think."

Having a credible referral makes such a difference in securing and succeeding with initial calls that it is worth considering not contacting a prospect at all without a referral. Regardless of what you sell and to whom, you can build a referral network that will turn cold calls into warm calls and put you on the fast track to achieving your sales goals. It is almost always possible to get a referral if you are determined to do so.

PRACTICE

Have you ever been on a call or in a meeting that just got off to the wrong start? When this happens it is often difficult to recover and leave a favorable impression. The initial minutes of a call or meeting are when the most is at stake. The client will have his detectors ready and will actively contemplate whether or not we are safe, worthwhile, and enjoyable to speak with, let alone do business with. What happens in the first five minutes of a call or meeting often has a big impact on the value of the remaining time; the authors call that time the High Risk Five. Some common errors that occur here are:

- Lack of preparation
- Last minute rehearsal
- Monologue vs. dialogue
- All about us
- Too long and detailed
- Not compelling

> ❖ Nowhere in the sales process do a few minutes of dialogue more quickly determine whether we continue or end our relationship than the initial interaction.

A superbly executed first few meetings can fast-track the opportunity and potentially distance us from competition. To execute well takes preparation and *practice.*

The most brilliantly delivered acting performances and speeches begin as a script. Actors turn the script into characters: they become the characters and the script is no longer apparent. Most consultants benefit from creating a script for the High Risk Five and practicing it until it is authentic and flows naturally. Here are steps to help make practice lead to successful and effective execution.

1. *Begin early.* It almost always takes more time than you expect to get it right.
2. *Write it.* Writing a meeting plan takes some time. However, it takes far less time to write a meeting plan than it does to pursue numerous low probability opportunities. Writing and executing a meeting plan will very likely help you to:
   - Exit low probability opportunities early.
   - Shorten the sales cycle.
   - Increase the win rate.
3. *Say it out loud.* Often what we write seems to flow and make sense, until we actually say it. Practice your script until it flows freely and naturally; ideally, practice with another person.

4. *Visualize success.* Have a successful call first in your imagination and then with the client. Imagine yourself talking with the client, either on the phone or in person, and pay close attention to what success looks like, sounds like, and feels like. Right before your actual meeting, re-create the look, sound, and feel of success. Begin the meeting with that state of mind and body. Visualize your success and you are likely to experience it more often.

Usually, in an opening statement we want to:

1. Connect personally.
2. Be clear about the purpose of the call.
3. Quickly create some curiosity or interest.
4. Transition to inquiry.

We then should be ready to address the key beliefs with proof or proposed action, resolve yellow lights if any, and execute the End in Mind.

Following is the opening statement from our initial meeting with NewLogo. The wording was crafted to meet the very direct style and language of the key executive:

> Thanks in advance for carving out two hours to meet with us today. I imagine that when we asked for two hours you might have been wondering how many PowerPoint slides we have. We have none. You might even expect us to go on and on about our company. We won't. Instead, we want to roll up our sleeves and work with you to size up a potential revenue recovery opportunity.
>
> The agenda we sent is intended to guide us toward identifying whether there is an opportunity or not. If there is, we will examine what the project entails and what it would cost. After covering these topics, there will either be something to pursue, or there won't. If there is, either you will like our help, or you won't. You mentioned you would be happy to let us know, one way or the other, at the end of our meeting today, and that works for us. While we would like to do business with you, if it's not in the cards—no harm done. We appreciate the opportunity to work with you today. Does that fit your sense of what you would like to accomplish?

Both of our companies did some homework so there are some things we know and some things we don't know. Would you mind if we start with a few questions?

PRE-POSITIONING MEETINGS FOR SUCCESS

Clients often come to meetings with consultants unprepared to use time constructively. They may have been sent an agenda recently, yet merely glanced at it. They may not receive an agenda until the beginning of the meeting. Or an agenda will not be offered at all. A meeting set up this way is often unproductive. In the best case, no one notices, and all that is lost is the opportunity to distinguish us and our company. This is nevertheless a big loss. In the worst case, the client perceives us as unprepared and unprofessional—and determines early not to work with us. Often people are polite and do not tell us what they really feel; instead, they say some version of "We will get back to you" or "Let's stay in touch." Nobody needs more of that. Pre-positioning sets up these meetings to be successful.

There are four key elements to pre-positioning.

1. Agreeing with the client on the End in Mind for the meeting.
2. Gaining an agreement that the agenda for the meeting is appropriate, complete, and, if covered, would actually enable them to execute the End in Mind.
3. Outlining what the client could do in advance to be well-prepared for the meeting.
4. Requesting information in advance that you might need to maximize the time.

The authors recommend sending an e-mail well in advance of the meeting covering these four points.

The e-mail sent to NewLogo was very close to the agenda described earlier, and invited the CFO to change it if he desired. The CFOs response to this e-mail was, "I think this is exactly what we should cover." When we arrived for the meeting, there was no surprise as to why we were there, what we planned to cover, and what decision was to be made. We followed the plan and left there with a verbal commitment to write a contract. Three weeks later the contract was signed and the engagement began. Traditionally the sales cycle had included numerous meetings and had taken six to twelve months. Working together, this sales cycle was successfully executed in fewer than sixty days.

This was possible because we:

1. Prioritized our list of prospects, which allowed us to pursue fewer opportunities and do them better.
2. Prepared a highly relevant business case hypothesis, based on an in-depth knowledge of the company and people we met with.
3. Personalized our approach by gaining a referral to the key stakeholder.
4. Practiced our Meeting Plan as a team well in advance of our call and meeting.
5. Pre-positioned our agenda prior to the meeting, so that the time we spent together was well used.

REVIEW

You can see in the graphic that follows what we have covered in this chapter.

Initiating New Opportunities

CONCLUSION

You can start with nothing other than willingness and this approach, and consistently end up with valuable new business—both with current clients and prospective ones. That is a powerful choice to have available. If you already have more new business than you can handle, or if you get up in the morning thrilled at the prospect of making cold calls, you won't need or want to exercise this choice. Should you choose to go down this path you will find that, like all new skills, you will improve with practice and experience. Your learning curve and results will accelerate if you choose to work with the authors, our colleagues, or other skilled professionals. That is not at all a necessity, just a reality. If you want to explore that possibility, give us a call. We're pretty easy to talk with.

LAST WORDS

My name is Randy Illig. Mahan began this book with a personal story of how it came to be in your hands. I will end it with one of my own. I began my selling career when I was seven years old. I answered an ad in the back of a comic book. It read something like this: "Earn gifts of your choice by selling flower and vegetable seeds to your neighbors." Seemed simple enough—I sell some seeds and I get a BB gun. A few weeks later my consignment of seeds arrived and I was a new representative of the American Seed Company; pretty good for a seven-year-old.

I immediately hit the streets knocking door to door, asking, "Wanna buy some seeds?" Some people said yes and some said no, but I sold enough seeds to get my own BB gun. This experience began my career in the rejection and reward game. I continued through my childhood and early adolescence to sell seeds and many other things advertised in comic books. Most ventures went well, others failed. Either way, I was learning a valuable lesson—people buy what they value. My job was to figure out what they value and then whether I could help or I couldn't—pretty simple. Even when I got out of school and hit the streets as a sales professional, I merely repeated this process and it served me well.

Fast-forward a few years and I find myself leading a company—CEO of a growing business. I felt personally responsible for 500-plus families. In order to fulfill this responsibility we needed to sell new work, every day.

While I understood what it would take to do that at the elemental level, I could not scale it. Enter, stage right, Mahan Khalsa.

I was looking for someone to help me turn the sales engine on, and I talked to the usual suspects. Nothing connected. Most of the "sales training" firms I talked to were too focused on the process of doing something *to* customers vs. *for* customers. Mahan was quite different. His sales approach to me made me feel understood and very open to his help. I thought to myself, *If only our sales people could do this.*

I engaged Mahan to help my company, and he served us well. He provided us with a replicable process and approach to "Helping our Clients Succeed." It worked! We grew like wildfire and the rest was history. In 2001 I joined Mahan at FranklinCovey's Sales Performance Group to teach others what Mahan had taught me. Together with our colleagues we have continued to propel our ability to help clients improve sales performance, both with new skills sets and new processes and tools.

So here is the juice: this stuff works! Not just in a book but in the field. It works for individuals and it can transform organizations. Imagine that in a few months—or at the outside, a year—you were achieving your "stretch" sales goals on purpose and with purpose. The journey begins with a simple step: start by freeing yourself from selling something and instead focus on understanding what problems your clients and prospective clients want to address and the results that they value. Mutually explore whether what you do well is a good fit for what they value. Use the structured conversation model to stay focused and productive. Codevelop a good up-front agreement about how decisions will be made and make sure to talk with the people who will make or influence them. These open discussions will lead to final presentations that enable winning decisions—for both you and your clients. Great rewards await you.

Many people choose to read a book and implement what they learned on their own. Others want help. If you are in the first group, know that many others before you have chosen this path and been successful. If you want some help, give us a call. Helping clients succeed is a passion for us, and we would enjoy the opportunity to talk. Even if you don't need help and are just willing to share interesting experiences, give us a call—we'd love to hear your side of the story.

APPENDIX ONE

SUMMARY AND QUICK REFERENCE

The pages in this appendix provide a quick overview of the material in the book. You may find it helpful to remove them from the book, carry them with you, and refer to them before you interact with a client. Or just bring along the book.

The ORDER of Successful Business Development

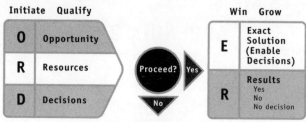

The Opportunity: You can't help somebody who has no perceived need.

Clarify the solution. Move off the solution. Structure the conversation: issues, evidence, impact, context, and constraints.

The Resources: You can't help somebody with insufficient resources.

Explore time, people, and money.

The Decision Process: You can't help somebody who cannot make a decision.

THE DECISION PROCESS				
Step	Decisions	When	Who	How (Criteria)
				Find out the How directly from the Who

The Exact Solution: Proposals don't sell—people do.

Present in person to the right people for the right amount of time in the right environment. Start with and gain agreement to the End in Mind. (What is reasonable for the client to say, do, or decide?) Articulate the key beliefs the client must resolve to comfortably and confidently decide the End in Mind. For each belief: provide proof/propose action; answer (the real) questions; ask for a decision with good EQ; resolve yellow lights.

Strongly connect what you heard and learned to what you present. How does your solution enable the Opportunity within the available Resources in a way that matches the Decision Criteria?

The Results: How you solve creates more sales than how you sell.

YES: Foresee and prevent potential problems up-front; follow through on creating a solution that exactly meets the client's needs. *NO:* Find out where and how you missed. *NO DECISION:* Go back to the decision process and define a discrete series of steps that would allow the client to say with confidence either Yes, let's do it, or No, thank you.

Getting in the Zone

1. **Intent Counts More Than Technique.** Your intent sets you free. It is difficult to excel at business development without being congruent and authentic.

    A.   What is your intent? What do you want the client to perceive about you and your purpose for interacting with them? Is your intent mutually beneficial?

    B.   Create a "resource state": what do you look like, sound like, feel like when you are 100 percent congruent and authentic with your intent?

    C.   Create an "anchor": develop a visual, auditory, kinesthetic (or multisensory) cue to associate with your resource state. Use repeatedly; build the association.

    D.   Before every client interaction, enter and communicate from your resource state.

2. **Know What Gear You're In.** Develop strong skills in each gear and be able to move knowingly and fluidly between them.

    Active Gear: The ability to manage resources to affect a result.

    Receptive Gear: The ability to understand what others think, feel, or believe to be true. See "Hints for Effective Questioning and Listening."

    Observant Gear: The ability to accurately perceive what is happening. (Green, Yellow, Red)

    The Law of Requisite Variety: The element in any system with the most flexibility, adaptability, choices will be the controlling element in the system.

3. **Check Your Ego at the Door.** Intent will set you free. Gear awareness will keep you flexible. Checking your ego keeps you clear-minded and fearless.

4. **Develop Conscious Competence.** Continually increase awareness of what is and what is not possible—of what works and what doesn't. Consistently add choices—skills, abilities, attitudes—that increase Business Intelligence (IQ), Emotional Intelligence (EQ), and Execution Intelligence (XQ).

Hints for Asking Effective Questions	Hints for Effective Listening
• Ask for permission to ask questions. • Ask one question at a time; wait for the answer. • Reward the response, then ask your next question. (When appropriate, use the client's words from their questions: it's a powerful reward.) • Be cautious of leading questions (questions designed to get agreement, not information or understanding). • Be aware of when "how" or "what" works better than "why." • Summarize: Did I get it right? Did I leave anything out?	• Listening is a matter of choice and concentration. Choice: You must choose to listen actively. Concentration: Focus your complete attention on the other person. • Focus on the client's answer, not on your next question. • Be aware of and lower your internal dialogue. • Listen with your ears, watch with your eyes, sense with your intuition the real meaning of the client's communication. Is there a difference between what was said and what was meant?

The Opportunity Overview

Context: Who or what else is affected? How does this opportunity tie into key strategies and initiatives?

Problem Evidence

Soft Issue: How, What, Where

How does the problem manifest?
What lets you know it's a problem?
Where do the effects of the problem show up?

Hard Issue: 5 Golden Questions:

1. How do you measure it?
2. What is it now?
3. What would you like it to be?

Results Evidence

Soft Issue: How, What, Where

How will we know we are successful?
What is your "punch list" for success?
Where will you see the benefits?

Hard Issue: 5 Golden Questions:

1. How do you measure it?
2. What is it now?
3. What would you like it to be?

Solution

Problem Impact

4. What is the value of the difference?
5. Over time? (2-3 years)
   Qualify: How important 1–10?

How much is this costing the organization?
($$$ or 1–10)

Results Impact

4. What is the value of the difference?
5. Over time? (2-3 years)
   Qualify: How important 1–10?

What is the payoff if success is achieved?
($$$ or 1–10)

Constraints: What has stopped the organization from addressing these issues? (What might stop them from successfully moving forward?)

List Key Issues (Prioritize!)

Problem/Result
Use a key word or phrase.

Problem = Pain
Result = Gain
Use their words

② Problems = challenges, issues, difficulties, concerns, dissatisfactions

Results = objectives, goals, outcomes, benefits, rewards

① You can test with the client additional problems/results from your experience.

Test for completeness: Solve these and nothing else = solution that exactly meets needs?

Summarize!
Did I get it right?
Did I leave anything out?

Opportunity Flow

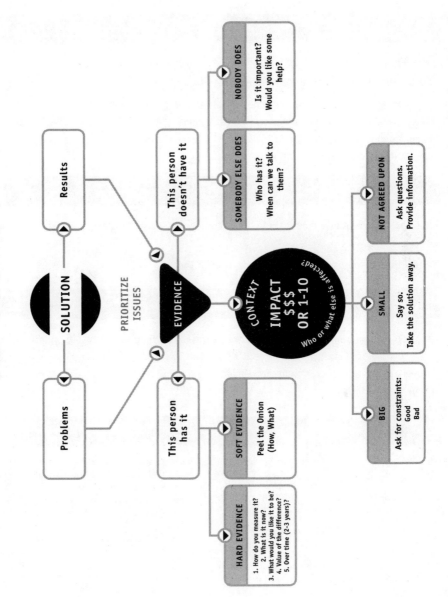

Resources

Start date: When are you hoping to get started on this project?

End date: How soon do you need the results in place?

Yellow lights: Too late, undefined time, or date too far in the future. (What makes it okay to waste more money?) Unrealistic or too short of a time frame. (What is driving that date? Is it worth more money to go faster? If they could really get the results they want and it absolutely requires more time, is it still worth discussing?)

Who does what: What are your thoughts as to how we should divide efforts between your people and ours?

Yellow lights: Too little of our involvement or of theirs.

Have you thought about what level of investment is appropriate for the results we discussed? (Have you established a budget for this project?) Our goal: Is the client's expected range of expenditure an overlap for our expected range of needed investment? If yes, we proceed. If no, we deal with it now rather than later.

Client Statement	Consultant Response
a. "No, we don't have a budget for this." b. "You tell me what this should cost" c. "It has to be self-funding." Or, "If it's worth it, we'll come up with the money." d. "I'd rather not (or can't) tell you." e. "It's part of a larger budget." f. They have a budget and it's too small, or their budget is lower than the range we offered.	**Answer for a, b, c, d, e:** I don't know how much this will cost you (every client situation is unique). Other companies in similar situations, achieving these kinds of results, tend to invest between X and Y. Can you see yourself falling somewhere in that range? **Answer for f:** And how did you come up with that number? If the answer is logistics, then deal with logistics. If the answer is value, then one of three things probably exists: (1) They don't believe in the value placed on the issues; (2) They don't believe you will deliver the results; (3) They believe someone else can deliver the results for less. Which is their belief?

Have You Thought About an Investment Amount?

Have you thought about what amount of investment
is appropriate for the results we discussed?

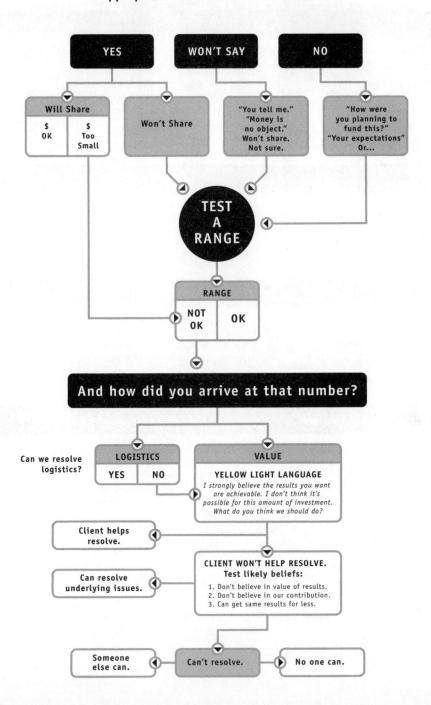

THE DECISION PROCESS				
Steps	**Decision**	**When**	**Who**	**How: Decision Criteria/Values**
What are all of the steps?	*What decision gets made in each step?*	*When will they decide?*	*Who is involved in each step?*	*Elicit the HOW (criteria) directly from the WHO.*
Are the steps logical, complete? Do they result in an ultimate Yes or No?	Sometimes the step and the decision are synonymous.	Set at least a tentative date for the decisions.	Who gets involved to make the decision in this step?	We want to interview the people who make or influence the decision in each step.
If we follow these steps will we be competitive?	Sometimes it is not clear what they will decide or influence in this step. Be clear.	If the decision process is long: how much of the impact value is lost or delayed?	Did we include everyone?	When we interview them we want to understand the Opportunity from their perspective; their Decision Criteria, and to test any yellow lights.
Would we suggest changes?		How does the timing here compare to the time they wanted to see the results in place (or get started)?	Do some votes count more than others?	How will they decide? Consensus? Many advise and one or few decide?
				See Gatekeeper Objections

Qualifying an Opportunity—20 Questions

Opportunity

1. What are all the issues the solution is intended to address? *Quick List*
2. What lets you know it's a problem? *Problem Evidence*
3. How much is this costing your organization? *Problem Impact*
4. How will we know we are successful? *Results Evidence*
5. What is the payoff if success is achieved? *Results Impact*
6. Who or what else is affected? *Operational Context*
7. What is the big picture? What is important to understand about your organization as a whole? *Organizational Context*
8. What has stopped your organization from resolving this in the past? What might stop your organization from achieving these results in the future? *Constraints*
9. Did I get it right? Did I leave anything out? *Summarize*

Resources

10. When are you hoping to get started on this project? *Time*
11. Do you have any thoughts about how we should divide efforts between your people and ours? (Look for a rough percentage: 70/30, 80/20, etc.) *People*
12. Have you established a budget for this project? *Money*

Decision Process

13. What are all the steps your organization will have to take to make a good decision in its own best interest? (Make sure yes or no is an okay outcome.) *Steps*
14. What decision gets made in each step? *Decisions*
15. When will each step take place? (You want at least a tentative date.) *When*
16. Who gets involved in each step? (Make sure it's complete.) *Who*
17. How will the decision makers decide? What criteria will they apply? *How* **Find out the how directly from the who.**
18. How will decision makers decide among alternative solutions? *Competition*
19. Who stands to gain or lose if this solution is adopted? *Gain/Loss*
20. How committed are you personally to resolving this issue? *Personal Stake*

Gaining Access: Our only goal is to produce a solution that truly meets yor needs. Based on what you've described, these people are key owners of those needs. For us to prepare a meaningful and relevant proposal, we'll need to talk to them. You know your company better than I, how do we set that up?

Gatekeeper	Resolve
They're too busy. ***It would take too much time.*** Acknowledge: I can appreciate how busy they must be... I can appreciate the pressure to use time well...	■ It won't take much time: 30 to 40 minutes each; we can do it on the phone if necessary. ■ If we make a presentation that doesn't address their priorities or criteria, that doesn't give them the information they need to make a good decision; it's a horrible waste of their time. They hate it. ■ It will take them a lot more time than 30 minutes to undo an ill-informed decision. ■ We're going to spend huge amounts of time preparing a solution —we're only asking a very small amount of time to make sure that solution truly meets your needs.
If we let you do it we'd have to let everyone do it and: ***1. ...that would take too much time.*** ***(and/or)*** ***2. ...that wouldn't be fair. We need to keep a level playing field.*** Acknowledge: I appreciate the pressure to use time well. I appreciate the desire to be fair.	Time: See above. In addition: if you don't have enough time, either: ■ Reduce the number of competitors—not the access to key stakeholders. ■ Take the time and do this right. ■ Agree that the final N companies can get full interviews. If we let you: ■ Heighten, don't eliminate differentiation among competition. ■ How solution providers use your time is a great way to judge them (i.e., how they sell is a free sample of how they solve). ■ Suggestion: Let each company follow its own course of action. Tell them you will judge them by the efficiency and efficacy of their approach. Fairness: ■ The goal is to be fair to a solution that meets your stakeholders' needs, not to a bunch of outside vendors. And it's not fair to expect you can exactly meet the needs of people with whom you've never talked. ■ We're going to spend thousands of person-hours preparing a solution—all we're asking for in exchange is 30 minutes of an individual's time to make sure the solution is relevant. Isn't that fair? ■ Suggestion: Only let people talk to the stakeholders who feel they need to—and judge them positively or negatively by how well they use your time. That's fair. ■ If they don't ask, they probably don't need the time.

Gatekeeper	Resolve
I'll do it for you... (continued) Acknowledge: I appreciate the offer. You've certainly been helpful so far.	If you came to my company and my job was to get you the information from our key stakeholders, I could guarantee you at least two things: 1. I'd do my absolute best – and yet the communication would be filtered – it would be less than the original. (Telephone game) 2. I would not ask the same questions as you would – you're the expert – so crucial information may not be communicated. Option: Do it together? Option: Start with just one person and expand one at a time?
Put your questions in writing. Acknowledge: I appreciate the offer.	• Takes longer. • Communication is less rich. Suggestion: I will write down my questions, give them in advance, and then we can have a 20 to 30 minute conversation. Does that make sense?
Put your questions in writing and I'll share the questions and answers with all vendors. (Also: **Go to the bidders' conference and ask your questions there.**) Acknowledge: Thanks for the offer. Can I share a concern?	• You have proprietary information, which we cannot disclose under strict penalty (NDA). • Our inquiry (analysis) process is proprietary to us and we don't share it with our competitors any more than you would with yours. • We only ask that what's fair for you is fair for us as well. • Our conversations will only take about 30 minutes. If you gain important insights from them, please feel free to share them with all the vendors.
It's my job. They delegated it to me. Acknowledge: I appreciate that. My goal is to support you in that responsibility.	The job we do reflects on you. ■ We present well, you look good. ■ We present poorly, you look bad... WHETHER THEY CHOOSE US OR NOT. Suggestion: Go together to one person at a time... Notion: You may find it informative and enlightening as well.
You can't. It's not allowed. **It's against our policy.** **They don't see consultants.**	Acknowledge: And probably for some very good reasons. Could you at least share with me the reasons?

The Purpose of a Presentation is to... Enable a Decision!

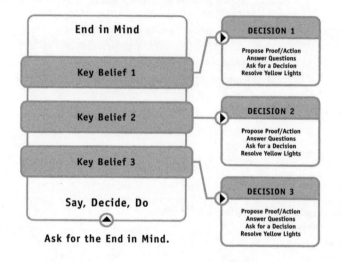

- **Present to the right people**
- **For the right amount of time**
- **With the right expectations**
- **In the right environment**
- **In the right competitive time slot**

MEETING PLAN	
End in Mind	At the end of the call, what do we want them to say, do, or decide? What will we say to introduce and position your EIM?
Key Beliefs	What key beliefs, intellectually and emotionally, must the client resolve to agree with the EIM?
Proof/Action	What will we do to address and satisfy the key beliefs?
Questions	Determine the questions we want to ask and how we will ask them. What will the client likely ask? How will we respond?
Yellow Lights	What are likely stalls, doubts, concerns, or objections? How will we respond?
Next Steps	What next steps might we suggest to the client at the end of the meeting?
Agenda	What is the agenda/critical path for the meeting? Can we get buy-in before the meeting?
Checklist for Success	❑ The intent driving our meeting is... ❑ Are the right people (client) attending the meeting? ❑ Do we have adequate time? ❑ Have we set the right expectations for the meeting? ❑ Our teams' roles and responsibilities are... ❑ Have we scrutinized our visual aides: easy to absorb? Support our EIM? ❑ Is the environment/venue appropriate? ❑ What topics, issues, questions, or behaviors are inappropriate for this meeting?

Yellow Lights

Questions: Make sure you answer the REAL QUESTION! It is often helpful to redirect the question posed before answering. The intent of redirection is to understand the real question, avoid answering the wrong question, and allow the other person to keep talking if that's what they really want to do.

Successful redirection=listening + softening statement + redirection question.

Nonprice Objections			
Match	**Understand**	**Resolve**	**Break/Substitute Equivalencies**
Acknowledge the statement or question.	Ask questions to discover the true concern or issue; find out what they mean by key words or phrases; elicit (when appropriate) their criteria for resolution (what would have to happen).	Work toward a mutual resolution of the true issue(s) at hand. If you can't resolve the issue, consider the following: change the relative importance of the criterion; show no one can meet the criterion; reframe the criterion.	Break/substitute equivalencies. If they want (or don't want) X, find out what X equals to them. Substitute: If we can give them what X equals, do they really need X? Break: Show how getting X won't give them what X equals; give counter examples.

Price Objections

A Framework for Price Negotiation

- ▶ Work for ART as if it were NoD
- ▶ Only negotiate price if it's the last issue.
- ▶ Offer options not ulitimatums
     (prepare in advance).
- ▶ The first options should keep you "whole."
- ▶ If you offer concessions:
     Concede slowly
     Concede small
     NEVER GIVE SOMETHING FOR NOTHING.
- ▶ Keep the Dialogue Open

Note: A prerequisite for Price Negotiations = Budget Cards

Gain Clarity on Next Steps

If no decision is made on the End in Mind, what specific steps will lead to that decision? If they ask you to "go away and do something," what happens if you produce what they want?

Use the "Never Do Something for Nothing" redirection:

- Define success: What specifically is needed in the future to make a good decision, and what are their success criteria for those actions/information?

- Verbally walk into the future: give them the ideal of what they want and ask, "Then what happens?"

- If the End in Mind decision is not "what happens," something is missing. What is it?

- Clarify what needs to happen to get to a Yes or No—and No is okay.

Results

- If at all possible, conduct a Win/Loss Analysis for the Opportunity.

- Whether the client responds with Yes, No, or No Decision, lay the groundwork for future business.

When the Decision Is Yes	When the Decision Is No	When the Decision Is No Decision
1. Make sure all yellow lights, present or future, are turned to green now while the relationship is strong. For an initiative like this, based on past experience: • What potential yellow lights might the client foresee? • What potential yellow lights might we foresee? • What preventive actions might we take? • What communication vehicles might we set up now to facilitate effective resolution of any difficulties in the future? 2. Do everything humanly possible to ensure they get the desired results (ideally, ones that can be measured).	Thank the client for their investment of time and energy. • Ask where your solution failed to meet their needs—or how some other solution was superior. • Plant the idea of us helping them: —If the current project doesn't work out. —On other projects.	1. Are there compelling reasons not to decide? • Is the business case no longer valid? (Has the evidence changed? Are they no longer experiencing the impact? Did the constraints go away? Did the context change?) • Do they not feel there is a solution that delivers the business case? How so? • Did priorities change? • Something else? 2. Elicit a concrete series of steps that will allow the client to feel completely comfortable saying either Yes or No—and No is okay. Follow the steps. Get a decision.

INITIATING NEW OPPORTUNITIES	
Prioritize	Do fewer, do them better. Select your top five prospects and invest 95 percent of your time in working with them. When one comes off the list replace it with the next priority prospect. Periodically review the list.
Prepare	Develop in-depth knowledge of the company and people you will call on. Prepare a Business Case Hypothesis (potential issues, evidence, impact, context, constraints). Prepare a Meeting Plan.
Personalize	No cold calls. Get a referral to the person you want to meet.
Practice	Rehearse what you will say and how you will say it. Rehearse your responses to potential questions and yellow lights.
Pre-position	Get agreement in advance for what will be a good use of time.

Initiating New Opportunities

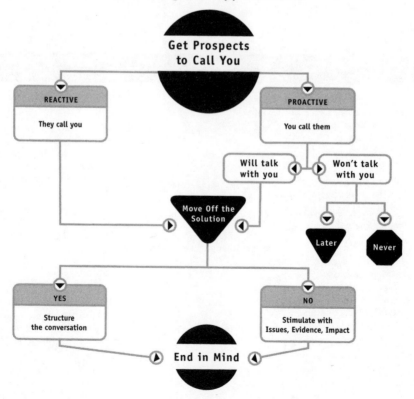

My Personal Success Criteria

What I will make sure to do in each of my client interactions:

What I will make sure I will not do:

APPENDIX TWO

CREATING AND APPLYING
AN INTENT STATEMENT

What is your intent as you work with clients—current or prospective? If it is not crystal clear to you, it may not be to them. The objective is to act congruently with that intent, so that people feel it even if they don't hear it spoken. When encountering communication difficulties, you may find stating your intent is helpful in establishing a common ground for resolution.

Intent is most powerful when it is mutually beneficial. The client will react to positively perceived intent, by divulging more of what they think, feel, and believe to be true. At the same time, you should feel that it is in your best interests, as well as theirs, if you are congruent with your intent. There is no need to eliminate nor conceal self-interest—only to align your self interest with theirs.

CREATE A "STATEMENT OF INTENT"

Here are some examples of a Statement of Intent:

- *My selling purpose* is to help people get the good feelings they want about what they bought and about themselves. (Larry Wilson & Spencer Johnson, *The One-Minute Salesperson*).

- My intent is to help you be more successful (Option: whether you choose to work with me or not).
- My intent is to help you be more successful in a way that enables us to enjoy the journey as well as the destination.
- My goal is to bring you excellent choices that would truly drive your success—whether you end up choosing us or not.
- My intent is to find out whether or not there is a good fit between what you value and what we do well. If so, I'll bring you good choices. If not, I'll be the first one to say so.

Please write out your "Statement of Intent." Feel free to use all, part, or none of the examples above. When finished, try it out with some friends or colleagues and get their reactions.

ACTING CONGRUENTLY WITH YOUR INTENT

Intent, as we use it, is not something we "put on" for the occasion. It is core to who we are and what we are about; it is revealed clearly when distractions and countervailing forces are removed. Though it is sometimes helpful to declare our intent, intent is conveyed by actions not by claims. Those actions in turn must be consistent and congruent. Congruent here is taken to mean alignment of the "four Vs":

Verbal: the actual meaning of your words
Vocal: how you say the words
Visual: how you look when you say the words
Visceral: a gut sense by others that you mean what you say—which is heavily influenced by the other three Vs.

If the Four Vs match each other, whether or not people agree with you, they will likely perceive you as congruent. And if you act consistently and congruently, people will believe your intent. (You still have to demonstrate expertise.) A powerful means of making intent happen on purpose is to build a resource state for intent. The tool of building a resource state can be used to call into being any peak performance state, not just intent. The process described below is derived from several authors of Neuro-Linguistic Programming (NLP), two examples of which are: Genie Laborde, *Influencing with Integrity*, and Anthony Robbins, *Unlimited Power*.

Step One: Introspect

Sitting peacefully by yourself, select a time in your mind when you are completely congruent with your intent. For these purposes, your brain does not care if the time is in the past, the present, or the future. What matters is that the experience be vivid. While completely congruent with your intent:

1. What do you look like? What are the features of your face, in detail? How do you hold your body? Note as much specificity as you can.

2. What do you sound like? What words do you use? How do you say them? What is the timbre, tone, and tempo of your voice?

3. What do you feel like? How does it feel in your body when you are completely congruent with you Intent? Connect strongly to those feelings and describe them as best you can.

If you are willing to take the time, repeat the above three steps for other instances of congruent intent. Reinforce, add definition, and gain clarity on "looks like, sounds like, feels like."

Step Two: Attach a "trigger" to your internal experience (or state) of being congruent with your intent.

A trigger is a mechanism that will "fire off" your desired internal state. A trigger can be:

- A kinesthetic action such as pumping a fist, rubbing your palms together, taking a deep breath, shaking your head, or any number of like actions
- A word or phrase you say to yourself
- A visual image you see in your mind's eye
- Some combination of the above

Fire the trigger, engage the state. Fire the trigger, engage the state. Repeat until strongly attached.

Step Three: Calibrate

Most people are not congruent with their intent, 24/7. It can be extremely helpful to consciously understand what, if anything causes you not to even enter your resource state for intent. What causes you to leave that state? What changes first? With increased awareness, often comes increased choice.

1. What might cause you not to enter or maintain your intent, even though you believe it is mutually beneficial to you and your client? What might you do to eliminate or reduce those influences should you so chose?

2. When you are congruent with your intent, and then not congruent, what changes? How you look? (If you were looking in a mirror, what changes would you notice?) How you sound? (If you were listening to a recording, what would you notice?) How you feel? (If you were "on the couch" describing your feelings, what would you say changed?)

Having gained the above awareness, what will you do when you notice the "signs of change" and want to stay congruent?

Step Four: Apply

Before you pick up the phone to talk with a client, or before you walk in the door to meet with them, fire your trigger and enter your resource state.

You may find it helpful to create a wallet-sized card or a sheet of paper you can easily reference in your planner or notebook with the following:

My Selling Intent:

Looks Like:

Sounds Like:

Feels Like:

Trigger:

APPENDIX THREE

GETTING PEOPLE TO CALL YOU

Getting people to call you means literally that your phone will ring and someone will be calling you with an idea that something you do might be helpful to them. The key is to build a strong referral network in your marketplace and be known as an expert, someone that people can reach out to. It takes some time to build a referral network, and it is worth every minute of the investment. People will call you and you will be able to make your sales goals with ease. In our opinion this is your responsibility—not the company you work for or the marketing department. Your referral network will be with you for life—you may have more than one employer, own your network. If you have no referral network start building one today—you will very likely see new leads within sixty days. Once built you will start receiving calls, and will make warm calls not cold calls. To get people to call you consider these ideas:

1. First, consider that some people like to refer other people to their friends and associates. Many of these people take pride in being a "go-to" source for "do you know someone who could help with _____? Your job is to find these people. Our experience is that a good referral source will have five or more potential clients call you each year. Imagine having five, ten, or fifteen of these relationships.

2. Become one of these people yourself. Find out who the best companies and people are who serve your market and recommend them. Get people to call you even if only to ask if you know someone who _____. After helping them, update them on what you are doing and remind them that you appreciate what they might send your way. It helps to be specific "I am focusing on helping midsized manufacturers get more cash out of operations by better managing finished goods inventory and raw materials on hand" vs. "Keep me in mind if you know of anyone looking for a new ERP system."

3. Identify the people you currently know who would be willing to refer you *and* have potential clients to refer to you. Contact each of these people and ask their permission to be in your referral network and be kept up to date on your business and how you are helping others get results. Keep in touch with these people. Sending six to ten e-mails and talking three to four times annually to each is a good target.

4. Once you have your list together make an appointment either in person or on the phone with each referral source. Focus on getting one strong referral at this meeting. Do this in addition to what is suggested in No. 3 above. When anyone makes a referral and someone calls you as a result—thank them immediately, even if you don't sell anything—try an old-fashioned handwritten note, a personal visit, or a phone call and a small token of appreciation if appropriate. When their referral leads to an order, follow up after you complete the work or fulfill the order and let them know how it went. Reward their help and they will likely do it again.

5. Constantly be on the lookout to add to your list. When someone referred to you buys invite them to participate in your referral network. Plan to spend twenty to thirty minutes each week working on expanding your referral network. Do it first thing Monday morning instead of 4 P.M. on Friday.

6. Make yourself known in the market you serve. Hang out where your prospects do. Join appropriate associations and become active as a speaker or volunteer. Remember—intent counts more than technique. Only sign on if you are willing to do so without expecting re-

turn. Serve the community and they will serve you. If speaking isn't for you, try writing. Contribute to the Web sites and publications that your clients value. Consider writing a column for your local newspaper. Become a "Web" personality: blogs, webinars, and podcasts are just a few of the many choices that are available when leveraging the Web.

Remember—this is about building your brand. We have talked with many successful salespeople who say that more than half of their business comes from people calling them. These ideas are some of the things that we have done ourselves or heard from others and know work.

ACKNOWLEDGMENTS

The authors, Mahan Khalsa and Randy Illig, accept full responsibility for the content herein. We cannot, however, accept full credit, for many reasons, among them the following.

Both of us are avid learners and continuously seek to augment our knowledge and skills. When we learn something that makes sense and is consistent with our values, we apply it. If it works, we reinforce and repeat. If it doesn't, we rip, reevaluate and replace. Thus our current state of the art is a synthesis of a lifetime of learning and application. To give full attribution to all the influences on this body of work would be a book in itself.

1. We work with incredibly capable colleagues at the FranklinCovey Sales Performance Group. They apply this body of work in over forty countries throughout the world, and their feedback and contributions are invaluable. Of particular note are contributions made by Scott Savage, David Marcum, Nicholas Harrison, Ian Edwards, and Michael Knowlton. Michael, in addition to his overall contributions, was seminal in developing the Initiating portion of this book.

2. Craig Christensen, a former colleague at FranklinCovey and a current partner with us in exciting new endeavors, continues to exert a strong positive influence both on our thinking and on how we work with clients in the field. He is not at all shy at breaking apart old

mental models and is especially adept and innovative in a way that encourages participation rather than resistance.

3. We work with top-notch global and regional companies. The professionals in these companies are smart. Most are eager to take their game to the next level, and most are aggressively impatient with anything that doesn't make sense or doesn't make a difference in increasing profitable revenue. Rightly so. We work with these professionals on real deals—in the classroom, behind the scenes, and in the field. Their intelligence, intuition, and experience about what works and what does not are inextricably woven into this book.

4. The current book benefits from previous iterations. In the mid-1990s, Mahan, with Gurucharan Khalsa, Ph.D., produced a book and coursework called *Asking Effective Questions.* In 1999 Mahan and FranklinCovey published the precursor of the current book, *Let's Get Real or Let's Not Play: the Demise of Dysfunctional Selling and the Advent of Helping Clients Succeed.* That book benefited from Mahan's field collaboration with Dick Carlson, author of *Personal Selling Strategies for Consultants and Professionals.*

5. You may encounter a book called *businessThink, Rules for Getting It Right—Now and No Matter What,* by David Marcum, Steve Smith, and Mahan. In part, *businessThink* was written in response to numerous requests from sellers to "teach this to buyers!" It is directed toward helping people in organizations make sound decisions. The similarity in content and language appropriately reinforces our belief that both buyers and sellers benefit from the same critical thinking, communication, and execution skills. What's good for one is good for the other. Should you decide to read both, be pleased rather than surprised by any overlap.

6. This book would not be a book without a superb team effort among many key players from FranklinCovey and Portfolio. From the FranklinCovey team, Sean Covey, Senior Vice President of Innovations and Products, gave the project a priority and provided flexible and creative business arrangements; Jeff Shumway, Vice President and General Manager of the Sales Performance Group, provided critical resources and support; Annie Oswald, Media

Product Director/Rights Manager, lent important focus and guidance; and Janita Andersen, Marking Manager of the Sales Performance Group, made countless contributions to details both small and mission-critical, for which we are immensely grateful. Our agent, Cheri Gilles, Director of Operations at Dupree/Miller & Associates, employed her vast experience to facilitate and coordinate the activities of the two teams.

At Portfolio, we are indebted to Adrian Zackheim, president and publisher of Portfolio, for his sponsorship, vision, and initiation of this project. Editorial director Jeffrey Krames was the orchestra conductor who not only kept everyone on the same page of music, he managed to blend many talented soloists into a group who played beautifully together. Jillian Gray, assistant editor, interacted with us the most. She jumped right into the trenches and worked with every word, concept, and flow of ideas. This is usually a thankless task. Let that not be the case here: we give Jillian heartfelt thanks.

On a more personal note, Mahan would like to deeply thank and acknowledge his wife, Annika Khalsa: Annika is my greatest teacher. Though I am a poor student, she has taught me much about honest, open, and meaningful communication. She encourages me to grow in every facet of my life. She has managed to open a heart in what used to be mostly intellect and willpower. This book would not be in your hands without her direct involvement. She has edited every word and composed many of them. Beyond burnishing rough edges, she has clarified concepts and stories, tested and refined ideas and language, and infused humor and freshness whenever possible. I am immensely grateful to share this adventure with her.

NOTES

KEY BELIEFS

Consultants and Clients Want the Same Thing

A recommended book is *Co-optition*, by Adam M. Brandenburger and Barry J. Nalebutt.

In an article entitled "Strategic Sales Management—A Boardroom Issue," by Benson Shapiro, Adrian Slywotzky, and Stephen Doyle, from *Harvard Business Review*, 1994, the authors contend that:

"Today the five key determinants of account profitability are:

1. Account retention
2. Account dominance emanating from the preferred vendor position
3. Realized price
4. Selling and service cost
5. Account selection

The single largest determinant of profitability in service businesses is account retention. . . . It also applies as much to product companies."

When we provide buyers with solutions that work, and do so in a way in which they appreciate the process as well as the results, they give us more business; we make more money. If we keep providing such solutions and they do more business with us than with any of our competitors, the amount of profit goes up. When clients perceive that our solution meets their needs better than their alternatives, we obtain a higher realized price. When we already have good relationships and are selling to people who like us, our selling costs go down.

It doesn't take professors from Harvard Business School to figure this out. It should be common sense. Yet often sellers concentrate on making a sale today rather than focus on a solution that exactly meets the client's needs—one that produces measurable value. When they do this, they make lower profits now and in the future. Committing to client success is good business.

BUILDING TRUST

Stephen M. R. Covey's book is *The Speed of Trust: The One Thing That Changes Everything*, written with Rebecca R. Merrill.

You can listen to a podcast of Mahan interviewing Stephen on the role of trust in sales by going to: http://franklincovey.com/SPG/podcasts/.

Stephen M. R. Covey talks about first building self-trust and extending it into relationship trust. To be trusted you must be trustworthy. One way to build trust in yourself and others is to make and keep commitments—to create an unbroken link between what you say and what you do. To create that link, as in building all desired habits, requires repetition and reinforcement. We literally carve new neural pathways in our brains and make those paths so well trodden that they become the default choice of the brain.

INCREASING SELF-TRUST

1. Pick a number of days that you will conduct this exercise. Be careful of the number you pick. If you pick it, do it. A suggested number of days to build a habit is thirty to forty. You might want to start with three days or five days, and then keep going.
2. Each day, make at least one personal commitment—something you will do or not do. Make the commitment out loud—voice it to the world. The key is, if you say it, do it. If you make a commitment, keep the commitment. You might want to start with a "slam dunk," such as: "I will get out of bed today." Embedding the pattern is more important than the degree of difficulty. As the pattern takes hold and your confidence increases, you can increase the commitment.
3. Many find it helpful to record the experience. You can do that in an experience journal or wherever it's convenient.
4. If something happens and you miss a day, or didn't keep the commitment, *start over*. Begin again at day one and complete the number of consecutive days you committed to. Gain insight and personal learning and build it into your growth. As long as you keep going, as long as you don't give up, there is no failure, just feedback.

INCREASING RELATIONSHIP TRUST

1. Be conscious of the commitments you make to clients. Don't say you will do something unless you can and will.
2. If you make a commitment, keep it. If you say it, do it. You may even want to record your experiences over a thirty- to forty-day period. Commit-

ments made, commitments kept. For the purpose of building the power of your word, there is no difference between big commitments and small commitments. You don't have to say, "I promise." Your spoken word is your promise.

3. Option: Mark out to the client your commitment and its completion. For example: "As we work together, I want you to know that if I say I'll do something, I'll do it, whether it is a small thing or a big thing. You said you wanted this information by Tuesday; I'll make sure you get it." When you send the report, you can preface it with, "As promised . . ." or "As you requested . . ." This should be "high EQ"—not self-serving or overdramatized, just an appropriately raised awareness. That which is not noticed may not be valued or might be taken for granted.

Another good book that deals explicitly with trust in sales is *The Trusted Advisor*, by David H. Maister, Charles H. Green, and Robert M. Galford.

Intent Counts More Than Technique

A good book that deals with intent is *You've Got to Be Believed to Be Heard*, by Bert Decker. Mr. Decker discusses the need to reach the "First Brain" of another person in order to get our message across to the "New Brain." Decker defines these as follows: "The First Brain is the nonreasoning, nonrational part of our brain. Simply put it is the seat of human emotion. The New Brain is the seat of conscious thought, memory, language, creativity, and decision-making." Mr. Decker contends that "our goal is to get our message across to the New Brain, because that's the decision-making part of our mind. But to reach the New Brain, our message must first pass through the First Brain, the emotional part of the brain." If the First Brain senses an adverse intent, the other person either may not hear what we have to say or may reject it out of hand.

Another good discussion of how the emotional part of our brain can highjack logic and reasoning is found in *Emotional Intelligence*, by Daniel Goleman.

The One-Minute Salesperson, by Larry Wilson and Spencer Johnson, is a short yet impactful book. Their concept of "selling on purpose" is very compatible with the notion that intent counts more than technique.

REACTANCE

For discussions on reactance and several additional sources on the topic, see *Resistance and Persuasion*, by Eric S. Knowles and J. A. Linn.

Solutions Have No Inherent Value

The exercise involving the assumptions embedded in the statement "The solution to the problem is" was stimulated by a workshop and workbook called "Precision Questioning" by Dennis Matthies of the Center for Teaching and Learning at Stanford University.

World-Class Inquiry Precedes World-Class Advocacy

Stephen R. Covey's *The 7 Habits of Highly Successful People*, an all-time business-book bestseller, is highly recommended. All seven habits apply to successful salespeople. The habits that follow are from Dr. Covey; the interpretations of their applications to sales are from us.

1. Be Proactive. Salespeople are famous for having excuses—there are many reasons outside their control to explain why sales aren't as good as expected or desired. Being proactive encourages us to take responsibility for what we *can* control, to increase our *response ability* ("Our behavior is a function of our decisions, not our conditions"). The short version for salespeople is focus on results, not excuses; focus on what you can do, not what you can't do.

2. Begin with the End in Mind. This habit suggests that we clearly and deeply understand what is truly important to us, what we value most. We can then assess if our activities and thoughts bring us closer to, or farther from, our life priorities. Beginning with the End in Mind is also based on the principle that all things are created twice: "There's a mental or first creation, and a physical or second creation to all things." In appendix two, the process of creating a resource state is a specific means of creating success first in your mind and then in execution. You'll also note that we use the concept of "Begin with the End in Mind" for presentations and meetings: we ask ourselves (and the client) what the client should be able to say, do, or decide at the end of our interaction. We then organize all that we do to enable that decision.

3. Put First Things First. Pareto's Law states that a small percentage of the inputs are responsible for a large percentage of the outputs; it is sometimes known as the 80/20 rule. In today's accelerated world, with its overwhelming amount of information and choices, we suggest the ratio should be 95/5: what is the 5 percent of activity that would most likely generate 95 percent of the desired results? Rigorous prioritization is essential for sales success. In initiating opportunities, do fewer and do them better. In qualifying opportunities, extract resources from low-probability opportunities and invest them in high-probability opportunities. In enabling decisions, give clients exactly what they need to decide on the End in Mind and nothing extra. In managing your personal time, focus on what matters most and assiduously eliminate distractions and less important uses of time.

4. Think Win-Win. This principle goes to the heart of intent. We are more

successful when we focus on helping clients succeed than when we concentrate on getting them to do what we want. We both need to win; however, if the client doesn't win, neither of us wins.

5. Seek First to Understand, Then to Be Understood. Seeking to understand (inquiry) is the essence of qualification. We are trying to create *mutual* understanding. Not only do we better understand clients, clients better understand themselves and what they really want; they *feel* understood. Seeking to be understood (advocacy) comprises the skills of enabling decisions. We help clients make good decisions in their own best interest.

6. Synergize. In order to get a "solution that exactly meets the client's needs," we need to be creative, flexible, and adaptable in matching what we do well to what the client wants and needs. It is likely we both will need to evolve our thinking and actions to get something that will truly work.

7. Sharpen the saw. Keep learning, keep growing.

LISTENING

The story about "If you hear it, you can play it" comes from *Everyday Zen*, by Charlotte Joko Beck.

There are many types of meditation. Those forms of meditation that increase your awareness of your internal dialogue can help you be a better listener. If there is no awareness, there is no choice. Here are two simple, yet powerful excercises you might find interesting and helpful.

Exercise one

Sit straight up in a chair, with your feet flat on the ground. Rest your hands comfortably on your thighs or intertwine your fingers and rest your hands in your lap. Keep your spine straight and your body relaxed. Close your eyes or open them slightly, looking down toward your hands.

Begin breathing with long, slow breaths. Allow the breath to primarily move in and out from the abdomen rather than from the chest. As you inhale, pay attention to your internal dialogue—to what is going on in your mind. Just take note without reacting or judging. You might even give a name to the thought— "Thinking of going to the store" or "Wondering how long I have been doing this"; again, just take note of what is showing up.

When you exhale, just relax your mind and let go of all thoughts. The thoughts may or may not release completely. No matter. Just continue to let go, to release. At some point the breath will be completely exhaled, and you will be ready to breathe in again. Right at the spot before you breathe in, enjoy a small taste of silence. When the breath naturally begins to return, repeat the process.

Be curious about how long you can continue the exercise without getting lost in your thoughts. Pay attention to your experience.

Exercise two

Sit and breathe as described in Exercise One. Count to ten, with a complete breath in and breath out signaling one number. For example, when breathing in, say to yourself the number one, breathing out say the number one. The next complete inhale/exhale will be number two. And so on. When you get to ten, start over at one and count to ten again.

See how many times, or for what period of time, you can count to ten without losing count. You may be surprised by how many times your internal dialogue causes you to lose track of your counting. If you can discipline yourself to remain focused on counting without losing your concentration, you will find that you will be better able to concentrate on exactly what the client is saying to you without being distracted by what you are saying to yourself.

Some additional books on listening include: *Listening: The Forgotten Skill*, by Madelyn Burley-Allen; and *The Wisdom of Listening*, edited by Mark Brady.

QUALIFYING: OVERVIEW

No Guessing

Sales Progression Index

The FranklinCovey Sales Performance Group and some of its clients use a Sales Progression Index (SPI) to measure the flow of meaningful information between client and consultant. Though an SPI can be used as a forecasting tool, its more important use is as a coaching tool. With an SPI, a sales leader can work with a salesperson on how to improve the flow of meaningful information as much as possible before presenting a solution. A small flow of information indicates a low-probability opportunity; we can offer gracefully to exit or proceed with caution.

An SPI is typically customized for a specific client and application. To give an idea of what one looks like, a generic version is shown on page 240, first as a one-page scorecard, and then with more detailed information. In this example, a sample mechanism for scoring the opportunity is given. Some clients like to give scores; others prefer not to use them.

Client: **Opportunity:**

	Date 1:	Date 2:	Date 3:	Date 4:
Person Interviewed..........4				
Opportunity (28)				
Issues.................6				
Evidence and Impact 12				
Context.................3				
Constraints 3				
Emotional Momentum......4				
Resources (8)				
Time 1				
People 1				
Money 6				
Decision Process (20)				
Grid 6				
Access 8				
Criteria 6				
SUBTOTAL 60				

Consultant:

	Date 1:	Date 2:	Date 3:	Date 4:
Exact Solution (20)				
Solution Advantage.......10				
Deal Advantage 4				
Relationship Advantage ...6				
Extra Advantage...........?				
Enabling Decisions (20)				
Format...................3				
Thought Structure 8				
Visual Presentation 2				
Yellow Lights, Nonprice 3				
Price Negotiation.............2				
Roles........................2				
SUBTOTAL 40				

TOTAL 100

SPI Sales Progression Index

Client Name: **Opportunity:**

Account Manager:

First Scoring: Date:	Second Scoring: Date:	Third Scoring: Date:

Highest Level of Person Interviewed

Rate the level of the person to whom you are talking. The scale represents a **continuous** *range of possible points.*

Who are you talking to? Just a blind RFP? Information gatherer? Technical person? Key influencer? Decision maker?	Blind RFP ....-4 Concerned stakeholder ....1 Strong influencer/decision maker.........4	Your Rating		
		Enter Date 1	Enter Date 2	Enter Date 3

IMPORTANT!!
The following information must come from
or be confirmed by the client.

The Opportunity (Client Confirmed)

Rate the opportunity in the following categories. A scale for each provides a **continuous** *range of possible points.*

		Your Rating		
		Enter Date 1	Enter Date 2	Enter Date 3
BUSINESS ISSUES. Have we tested that *all* the problems/results are being addressed? Are the issues prioritized by stakeholder? Does the client deem them meaningful and compelling?	Unconfirmed, vague, conflicting, uncompelling ....-4 Generic, predictable ....1 Complete, prioritized, compelling 6			
EVIDENCE AND IMPACT. Is the evidence for key issues hard, soft, nonexistent? Is there a monetary impact that the client agrees to? Is the impact large relative to the potential investment? How important is the impact to the client, from 1-10?	Missing or weak evidence/impact ..-4 Not available; willing to develop evidence/impact ....1 Hard evidence and substantial economic impact 12			

Continued: The Opportunity (Client Confirmed)

CONTEXT (OPERATIONAL AND ORGANIZATIONAL). Has the client identified who or what else is affected operationally? Do the issues tie into key organizational priorities?	Neither org or op. ....-2 Either org or op................................ 2 Both org and op............................... 3			
CONSTRAINTS (CONFLICTING PRIORITIES, POLITICS, RISK, RESISTANCE TO CHANGE, NEGATIVE BELIEFS, ETC.). What has stopped them from doing this in the past? What might stop them in the future? Can we/they deal effectively with these constraints?	Opportunity threatening constraints ....-8 Constraints not identified................. 0 Constraints identified and manageable...................................... 3			
EMOTIONAL MOMENTUM (COULD EXIST EVEN WITHOUT SOLID BUSINESS LOGIC). On a scale of 1-10, with 10 being "mission critical" and 1 being "who cares?" how important is this initiative to key stakeholders? How emotionally vested are they?	Who cares? (0-6)............................-6 Strong interest (7)............................ 1 Mission critical (8, 9, 10).................. 4			
	TOTAL			

The Resources (Client Confirmed)

		Your Rating		
Rate the opportunity in the following categories. A scale for each provides a **continuous** *range of possible points.*		Enter Date 1	Enter Date 2	Enter Date 3
TIME. Is the desired time frame reasonable, too short, or too distant/vague?	Opportunity-threatening time problems...-3 Time reasonable............................... 1			
PEOPLE. Are there reasonable attitudes and commitments regarding division of labor? Will the client commit the "right" people resources?	Opportunity-threatening people problems...-3 People reasonable 1			
MONEY. Are we and the client thinking similarly on the rough range of investment required to achieve the results? Is the money available?	Opportunity-threatening money problems...-6 Money has been qualified and is available 6			
	TOTAL			

Decision Process (Client Confirmed)

Rate the opportunity in the following categories. A scale for each provides a **continuous** range of possible points.		Your Rating		
		Enter Date 1	Enter Date 2	Enter Date 3
DECISION PROCESS. Have we mapped out with the client the STEPS, DECISIONS, WHEN, WHO? Are they complete? Reasonable? Favorable?	Client unresponsive or process is dysfunctional....................................-4 Steps only defined...........................1 Complete process defined and reasonable..6			
DECISION ACCESS. Is access to influencers and authorizers open or restricted?	All access denied ....-4 Partial but helpful access ....2 Everyone we want to see 8			
DECISION CRITERIA (FOR ISSUES, SEE OPPORTUNITY). Are the stakeholders willing and able to articulate their criteria for deciding between alternatives (do nothing, do it internally, choose us or someone else)? Can we meet the criteria?	Unwilling/unable to articulate, or adverse criteria...............................-4 Known and neutral ....0 Known and favorable.......................6			
	TOTAL			

Total ORD Rating		Your Rating		
		Enter Date 1	Enter Date 2	Enter Date 3
For the date specified, add the totals from each column for O, R, D, and the score for highest-level person interviewed.				

> **IMPORTANT!!**
> **The following information is a composite of our own beliefs**
> **and the opinions we've elicited from the client.**

Competitive Advantage/Competition includes: do nothing; do it themselves; do it with someone other than us.				
Rate the competitive advantage in the following categories. A scale for each provides a **continuous** range of possible points.		**Your Rating**		
		Enter Date 1	Enter Date 2	Enter Date 3
SOLUTION ADVANTAGE. How well does our solution produce the desired results? How does it rate for feasibility, ease of implementation, and perceived risk? How well does it meet the timing and the decision criteria? How does our solution compare to the alternatives?	Competition holds advantage (or our solution weak).....................-6 Perceived parity .... 0 Our solution is very sound and superior to competition 10			
DEAL ADVANTAGE. How does our deal structure compare to the alternatives? Pricing? Cash flow? ROI? Risk mitigation? Operational or financial flexibility? Strategic, tactical, competitive, other advantage for client?	Competition holds advantage (or our deal structure is weak)........-4 Perceived parity.............................. 0 Our deal structure is very sound and superior to competition 4			
RELATIONSHIP ADVANTAGE. How strong and positive is our personal, political, and professional relationship with key influencers and decision makers? If we have champions or supporters, what is their relative decision-making power?	Competition holds advantage (or our relationships are weak).......-6 Perceived parity.............................. 0 Our relationships are very strong and superior to competition 6			
EXTRA ADVANTAGE. Are there special considerations or circumstances that would favor either us or the competition?	Competition holds advantage.........-4 Perceived parity.............................. 0 Our advantage............................... +5			
	TOTAL			

Enabling Decisions

Rate your (or your team's) ability to present to enable decisions in the following categories. A scale for each provides a **continuous** range of possible points.		Your Rating		
		Enter Date 1	Enter Date 2	Enter Date 3
PRESENTATION FORMAT. Are we presenting in person, to the right people, for the right amount of time (and in the desired position if competitive)?	Decision-threatening problems........-4 Challenging but doable...................0 Favorable...3			
THOUGHT STRUCTURE (THE LOGICAL AND EMOTIONAL ORGANIZATION THAT ENABLES A DECISION). Is it crystal clear which decision(s) the presentation is intended to enable? Will the client readily agree? Have we identified and organized around the key beliefs/supporting decisions the client must resolve to make the final decision(s)? Do we have compelling proof? Do we know how we will ask for the decision on both the supporting and ultimate decisions? Is the presentation flow logical, easy to understand, and involving?	Weakness exists ....-3 Reasonable yet needs work............0 Cogent, concise, compelling 8			
VISUAL PRESENTATION. Is the visual presentation easy to absorb? Does it complement and facilitate the thought structure?	Poor...-2 Acceptable.......................................0 Excellent..2			
NONPRICE YELLOW LIGHTS (STALLS, DOUBTS, QUESTIONS, OBJECTIONS). Have we foreseen and thoroughly prepared for the most likely questions, stalls, doubts, objections? Are we skilled in resolving unforeseen yellow lights?	Unprepared.....................................-2? Acceptable.......................................0 Well prepared 3			
PRICE NEGOTIATION (INCLUDES TERMS AND CONDITIONS). Do we have aggressive, realistic targets (ART)? Have we established the no-deal point (NoD)? Do we have options that would keep us "whole"? If we choose to move off ART, do we have options that we can trade off? Are we committed to not giving something for nothing? Have we prepared for predictable client tactics?	Unprepared......................................-2 Acceptable.......................................0 Well prepared 2			

Continued: Enabling Decisions				
ROLES. If more than one person is presenting, does everyone know their roles and objectives? Is there an "orchestra conductor"? Do we really need each person to accomplish the End in Mind? Is each fully prepared?	Poorly defined ....-2 Acceptable.. 0 Well orchestrated 2			
	TOTAL			

Total ORD + Person Interviewed + Competitive Advantage + Enabling Decisions Rating	Your Rating		
	Enter Date 1	Enter Date 2	Enter Date 3
ORD, including person interviewed			
Competitive Advantage			
Enabling Decisions			
TOTAL			

QUALIFYING OPPORTUNITIES

One research firm estimates that 65 percent of salespeople are pursuing worthless deals. How productive is that? Eighty percent of lost sales opportunities are a result of an inadequate or nonexistent qualification process and the lack of an effective sales planning process. (ES Research Group, Inc., www.ESResearch.com)

Context: Two Types

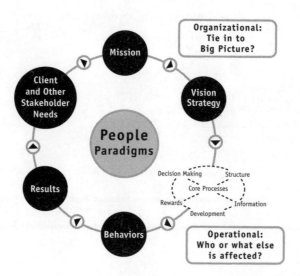

One of the tools FranklinCovey uses to help consultants think systemically is the Organizational Effectiveness Cycle™ (OE Cycle). To achieve their economic and service mission, leaders in an organization establish strategies and prioritize key initiatives. Based on their beliefs about what causes others to make those strategies a reality, they put in place what they feel are the "Six Rights":

1. The Right Processes
2. The Right Structure
3. The Right People
4. The Right Information
5. The Right Decisions
6. The Right Rewards

Leaders and managers presume the Six Rights will motivate and enable people to produce the results desired by key stakeholders inside and outside the organization. If the results are not achieved, one or more of the Six Rights isn't right.

For instance, if we were installing a new information system, we would interview key stakeholders about the results they wanted from getting the right information. Yet even if we were to put in the world's best information system, the organization may not get the desired results unless: the information were properly integrated into how they do business (their processes); people were rewarded for inputting and using the information and trained to do so; people were allowed to make appropriate decisions based on the new information; and the structure of the organization was aligned with how the information could best be used.

Likewise, let's say we put in a sales training program designed to improve specific results. Even if the program is superb and highly rated by the participants, will those results be sustained over time if no changes are made to the organization's other systems and processes? If the organization doesn't reward people for performing what they learned, will they improve? If they don't give the people trained the right information to execute and monitor performance, will they succeed? If they don't allow their people to make the appropriate decisions, will new skills even matter? If they don't examine how they structure territories, working relationships, and interactions with other parts of the company, will new behaviors be sustainable? If they don't increase other competencies and knowledge apart from business development skills, is it likely they will achieve the full potential of the desired results?

When clients get solutions that work, we benefit. They give us more business. To make solutions work, it is helpful to think holistically, systemically. Who and what else need to be aligned with our solution for clients to get the results they want. Will they align those elements themselves, or do they need some help? If they need help, can we help them? If not, do we know someone who can?

A good book on systems thinking is *The Fifth Discipline: The Art and Practice of the Learning Organization*, by Peter Senge.

Constraints

A great little book on "getting real" and recognizing, understanding, and dealing with constraints in organizations is *Overcoming Organizational Defenses: Facilitating Organization Learning*, by Chris Argyris.

QUALIFYING DECISIONS

See also Dr. Paul C. Nutt, *Making Tough Decisions* (New York: Jossey-Bass, 1989).

WINNING: THE ART OF ENABLING DECISIONS

The ability to enable decisions coalesces many skills and abilities. Following are some recommended sources.

Key Beliefs

A great discussion on how beliefs work—and don't work—to get us what we want, is *The 10 Natural Laws of Successful Time and Life Management: Proven Strategies for Increased Productivity and Inner Peace*, by Hyrum Smith. See his discussion of the Reality Model in Laws six, seven, and eight.

Logic (IQ)

The Pyramid Principle: Logic in Writing and Thinking, by Barbara Minto.
Being Logical: A Guide to Good Thinking, by D. Q. McInerny.
ETC: A Review of General Semantics, The Institute for General Semantics (2004–2008) and the International Society of Semantics.

Emotion (EQ)

How to Argue and Win Every Time, by Gerry Spence.
You've Got to Be Believed to Be Heard, by Bert Decker.
Influence: The Psychology of Persuasion, by Robert B. Cialdini.
Influencing with Integrity: Management Skills for Communication and Negotiation, by Genie Z. Laborde

Presentation and Facilitation Skills (XQ)

"Presentation Advantage," a course by FranklinCovey.

For facilitation skills find a good course on group facilitation skills—one that goes beyond "flip chart art" and teaches you how to work effectively with groups of people

Resolving Yellow Lights

Resistance and Persuasion, by Eric S. Knowles and J. A. Linn.
The Story Factor: Inspiration, Influence and Persuasion Through the Art of Storytelling, by Annette Simmons.
Crucial Conversations, by Kerry Patterson, Joseph Grenny, Ron McMillan, and Al Switzler.

Personality Styles

The authors chose not to engage the topic of personality styles in this book. Many people find them useful in designing their presentations and interactions to match the particular personality style of the clients they work with. Many of today's popular style systems derive from the psychological theories of Carl Jung and perhaps go even further back to the four temperaments or four humors of the ancient Egyptians and Greeks. Almost all have four primary styles, pictured in four quadrants, which can be further segmented into sixteen.

Each style system has its own advocates and devotees. Two that the authors and some of their clients have worked with are:

People Styles at Work: Making Bad Relationships Good and Good Relationships Better, by Robert Bolton and Dorothy Gover Bolton.

The Color Code, by Taylor Hartman, Hartman Communications.

Another popular model is the Myers-Briggs Type Indicator (MBTI) personality inventory.

Negotiation

FranklinCovey Sales Performance Group offers a course in negotiation that integrates well with this book. In addition, the authors highly respect the various works of Robert Fisher (professor and Director of the Harvard Negotiation Project) and William Ury, two of their more popular are *Getting to Yes*, and *Getting Past No*.

Another good book is *The Mind and Heart of the Negotiator*, by Leigh Thompson.

Results

We recommend the body of work by Fred Reichheld, in particular *The Ultimate Question: Driving Good Profits and True Growth*. The ultimate question is, "How likely is it that you would recommend this company to a colleague or friend." The answer to this question drives what Fred terms the Net Promoter Score: "Net Promoter Score (NPS) is based on the fundamental perspective that every company's customers can be divided into three categories. Promoters are loyal enthusiasts who keep buying from a company and urge their friends to do the same. Passives are satisfied but unenthusiastic customers who can be easily wooed by the competition. And detractors are unhappy customers trapped in a bad relationship." NPS is calculated by subtracting detractors from promoters.

The idea of running your business to create net promoters is completely aligned with the selling process of Helping Clients Succeed. This book and process are also an excellent fit for creating referrals on purpose.

INITIATING NEW OPPORTUNITIES

The percentages on how often people will agree to meet with you if you have a referral come from: "Selling to Senior Executives: How Salespeople Establish Trust and Credibility with Senior Executives," a white paper written by Alston Gardner, chief executive officer, Target Marketing Systems, Inc.; Stephen J. Bistritz, EdD, director of development, Target Marketing Systems, Inc.; and Jay E. Klompmaker, PhD, professor of business administration, Kenan-Flagler Business School, University of North Carolina.

The quote on account retention is from "Strategic Sales Management: A Boardroom Issue," by Benson Shapiro, Adrian Slywotzky, and Stephen Doyle, in *Harvard Business Review*, 1994.

In Appendix Three we suggested some ideas to get people to call you. John Jantsch of Jantsch Communications has taken ideas like these and built an easy-to-implement "system" for marketing yourself and your business, and for getting people to call you. John's book *Duct Tape Marketing* and his "Referral Flood" program outline one approach to building a strong referral network. There are five key steps to John's Referral Flood.

Step 1—Create a referral target market.
Step 2—Design a referral education system.
Step 3—Outline your referral lead offer and system.
Step 4—Create a referral conversation strategy.
Step 5—Identify a referral follow-up strategy.

This straightforward program can be ordered from Duct Tape Marketing and implemented with ease. For more information, visit www.ducttapemarketing.com.

Never Eat Alone by Keith Ferrazzi, is a great book and a must-read if you have an interest in building your network. Also, as mentioned earlier *The Ultimate Question*, by Fred Reichheld, is a powerful complement to building referrals on purpose.

A topic we did not include in this book is "drip marketing" or "permission marketing." When we initiate an opportunity with prospective clients, they will either choose to pursue it at that time or choose to decline. If they choose not to pursue it at the particular time we meet with them, there may well be a future time at which they would be eager to explore our solutions. Rather than be "one and done," we can keep our name in their awareness with a consistent communication that offers information they are likely to value.

For conducting research on your prospects, consider:

Onesource.com: OneSource's in-depth company profiles help you save time

researching corporate families, industries, key executives, and financial information and offers access to over 17 million global companies and 21 million executive profiles.

Hoovers.com contains insightful information about industries, companies,
and the people who lead them.

FinListics Solutions' innovative software programs allow sales professionals
to demonstrate a tangible return on investment and effectively communicate
how their solution can impact a customer's bottom line. www.finlistics.com

iProfile provides sales and marketing the information needed to create demand, qualify accounts, penetrate new accounts, and accelerate sales. iProfile answers the questions: Who are the people in IT, what is their contact information,
what are their titles, and to whom do they report? In addition iProfile provides
in-depth background information including biographies of key players and interviews as well as major application infrastructure and financials. www.iprofile.com

First Research is an industry intelligence company that helps sales teams perform faster and smarter, open doors, and close more deals. First Research per-
forms the "heavy lifting" by synthesizing hundreds of sources into an easy to
digest format a salesperson can consume very quickly to better understand a
prospect's or client's business issues. First Research updates each Industry Profile
quarterly and pushes out Email Alerts to ensure content is both timely and top of
mind. Customers include leading companies in banking, technology, telecom-
munications, business process outsourcing, and professional services such as
Bank of America and Merrill Lynch. Used by over 50,000 sales professionals, First
Research can benefit any organization that has prospects in multiple industries.
www.firstresearch.com.

About the Authors

MAHAN KHALSA is the founder of the FranklinCovey Sales Performance Group. Mahan is a world-renowned expert in business development and business-to-business sales. His clients have included Accenture, Aon, EDS, Microsoft, Oracle, and many others. Mahan is a highly sought-after speaker, author, and business consultant who has helped clients win billions of dollars in sales. He graduated with honors in economics from UCLA and has an MBA from Harvard. Mahan is a founder and partner in the company ninety five 5, LLC, a FranklinCovey joint venture.

RANDY ILLIG is a senior consultant at the FranklinCovey Sales Performance Group (SPG). Randy joined the SPG team because of his firsthand experience and success with the group's Helping Clients Succeed™ (HCS) sales process. He now trains, consults, and coaches clients on how to win more profitable business by using the HCS sales process. Randy is a partner with ninety five 5, LLC, a FranklinCovey joint venture and serves as its CEO. He is a former recipient of the Ernst & Young Entrepreneur of the Year award, the Ernst & Young "CEO Under 40" award, and the Arthur Andersen Strategic Leadership Award.

About FranklinCovey

FRANKLINCOVEY (NYSE:FC) is the global leader in effectiveness training, productivity tools, and assessment services for organizations and individuals. FranklinCovey helps companies succeed by unleashing the power of their workforce to focus on and execute top business priorities. Clients include 90 percent of the Fortune 100, more than 75 percent of the Fortune 500, and thousands of small and mid-sized businesses, as well as numerous government entities and educational institutions. Organizations and individuals access FranklinCovey products and services through corporate training, licensed client facilitators, one-on-one coaching, public workshops, catalogs, and more than eighty retail stores. FranklinCovey has nearly 1,500 associates providing professional services and products in the United States and in 35 international offices serving more than 140 countries.

About the FranklinCovey Sales Performance Group

The FranklinCovey Sales Performance Group (SPG) specializes in customized sales training, consulting, and coaching, and shows clients how to dramatically improve sales by becoming totally client-centered. SPG helps clients execute and build capabilities around effective sales planning and processes, sales leadership, sales management, and consultative selling skills. SPG's Helping Clients Succeed™ sales process breaks down dysfunctions in selling and buying and gives sales professionals the strategies, tools, and skills to become trusted advisors in the eyes of their clients. The process is based on the book *Let's Get Real or Let's Not Play: Transforming the Buyer/Seller Relationship*, by Mahan Khalsa and Randy Illig.

Products and Services

To learn more about relevant products and services, please call 800-707-5191 or 801-216-0004, or go to www.franklincovey.com/spg.

INDEX